ADVANCES
IN
TOUCH

ADVANCES IN TOUCH

New Implications in Human Development

**Edited by
Nina Gunzenhauser**

**Introduction by
T. Berry Brazelton, M.D.
and
Tiffany M. Field, Ph.D.**

Sponsored by

Johnson & Johnson
CONSUMER PRODUCTS, INC.

Library of Congress Cataloging in Publication Data
Main entry under title:

Advances in Touch: New Implications in Human Development

   (Johnson & Johnson Consumer Products, Inc. pediatric round table series: 14)

   Summary of a conference held May 1989 in Key Biscayne, Florida

Includes bibliography.
   1. Child development – Congresses. 2. Touch – Psychological aspects – Congresses.
3. Infants – Care and hygiene – Congresses. 4. Touch – Therapeutic use – Congresses.
I. Gunzenhauser, Nina. II Johnson & Johnson Consumer Products, Inc. III. Series:
Johnson & Johnson Pediatric Round Table series (Skillman, N.J.): 14. [DNLM: 1.
Child Development – Congresses. 2. Infant, Newborn – Congresses. 3. Infant,
Premature – Congresses. 4. Parent-Child Relations – Congresses. 5. Physical
Stimulation – Congresses. 6. Touch – Congresses. WS 105 A2446 1989]

RJ131.A384   1990   155.4'12182 – dc20

ISBN 0-931562-16-3

Cover photo: Art Kane

To James E. Burke
Chairman Emeritus,
Johnson & Johnson

His vision and strong leadership of Johnson & Johnson, so clearly evident during the Tylenol crisis, are broadly known and appreciated. Not so well known is his long standing commitment to a better understanding of the dynamic role of touch in human development.

For over thirty years, his inspiration and guidance within Johnson & Johnson have paralleled the work of scientists in offering parents and babies new insights into the value of touch as a modality for communication and attachment. We are indebted to him for his support of this and other conferences, which have allowed men and women from all disciplines to communicate and share our views and our information to foster a better understanding of touch and all that it represents.

CONTENTS

PARTICIPANTS

Catherine M. Balkunow
Marketing Communications
Johnson & Johnson Consumer
    Products, Inc.
199 Grandview Road
Skillman, New Jersey 08558

**Ronald G. Barr, M.A., M.D.C.M.,
F.R.C.P.(C.)**
Child Development Program
Room C-641
Montreal Children's Hospital
2300 Tupper Street
Montreal, Quebec H3H 1P3
Canada

T. Berry Brazelton, M.D.
Professor Emeritus
Harvard Medical School
Boston, Massachusetts 02115

Audrey K. Brown, M.D.
State University of New York
Health Science Center at Brooklyn
450 Clarkson Avenue
Brooklyn, New York 11203-2098

Helene C. Carty
Director, Consumer Relations
Johnson & Johnson Consumer
    Products, Inc.
890 Woodlawn Road West
Guelph, Ontario N1K 1A5
Canada

James T. Dettre
Consultant, Marketing
    Communications
Johnson & Johnson Consumer
    Products, Inc.
199 Grandview Road
Skillman, New Jersey 08558

Laurie Evans, M.A.
Instructor Trainer
International Association of
    Infant Massage Instructors
111 Hicks Street, Apt. 11G
Brooklyn, New York 11201
National Headquarters:
P.O. Box 16103
Portland, Oregon 97216-0103

Tiffany M. Field, Ph.D.
Department of Pediatrics
University of Miami
School of Medicine
P.O. Box 016820
Miami, Florida 33101

Jeffrey D. Fisher, Ph.D.
Department of Psychology, U-20
University of Connecticut
Storrs, Connecticut 06268

Jacob L. Gewirtz, Ph.D.
Department of Psychology
Florida International University
University Park Campus, DM 430
Miami, Florida 33199

Nina Gunzenhauser
Science Writer
P.O. Box 111
Franklin, New York 13775

Brian Healy, Ph.D.
Behavioral and Developmental
    Pediatrics
The Evanston Hospital
2650 Ridge Avenue
Evanston, Illinois 60201

Patricia Heidt, Ph.D., R.N.
Division of Nursing
State University of New York
    at New Paltz
New Paltz, New York 12561

John H. Kennell, M.D.
Department of Pediatrics
Rainbow/Children's Hospital
Case Western Reserve University
2074 Abingdon Road
Cleveland, Ohio 44106

Cassie Landers, Ed.D., M.P.H.
Consultive Group on Early
  Childhood Care and Development
UNICEF
Box H-11-F
Three United Nations Plaza
New York, New York 10017

Sandra K. Larson, Ph.D.
Mailman Center for Child Development
University of Miami
School of Medicine
P.O. Box 016820
Miami, Florida 33101

Brenda Major, Ph.D.
Department of Psychology
Park Hall
State University of New York
  at Buffalo
Amherst, New York 14260

Dorothy D. Matsu
Consultant, Marketing Services
Johnson & Johnson Consumer
  Products, Inc.
199 Grandview Road
Skillman, New Jersey 08558

Michael J. Meaney, Ph.D.
Douglas Hospital Research Centre
6875 Boulevard Lasalle
Quebec H4H 1R3
Canada

Jules Older, Ph.D.
Coordinator of Human Behavior
University of Vermont
College of Medicine
194 S. Prospect Street
Burlington, Vermont 05405

D. Kimbrough Oller, Ph.D.
Mailman Center for Child Development
University of Miami
School of Medicine
P.O. Box 016820
Miami, Florida 33101

Bonnie J. Petrauskas
Communications Administrator
Johnson & Johnson Consumer
  Products, Inc.
199 Grandview Road
Skillman, New Jersey 08558

Martin Reite, M.D.
Department of Psychiatry
Box C268R
University of Colorado
Health Sciences Center
Denver, Colorado 80262

Robert B. Rock, Jr., M.A., M.P.A.
Consultant, Professional Relations
Johnson & Johnson Consumer
  Products, Inc.
8742 Bald Eagle Lane
Wilmington, North Carolina 28405

Saul M. Schanberg, M.D., Ph.D.
Department of Pharmacology
Duke University Medical Center
Durham, North Carolina 27710

Sandra J. Tribotti, M.N., R.N.C.
Neonatal Nursing Consultant
4710 Burke Avenue North
Seattle, Washington 98103

Edward Z. Tronick, Ph.D.
Chief, Child Development Unit
The Children's Hospital
300 Longwood Avenue
Boston, Massachusetts 02115

PREFACE

As part of Johnson & Johnson's sustained commitment to the concept that the sense of touch is the foremost channel for infant and child development, the company directed the fourteenth of its series of Pediatric Round Tables to review the latest scientific progress in the field. The stimulus for the conference was the desire to know what research developments had taken place since the 1983 Round Table, "The Many Facets of Touch." Tiffany M. Field, Ph.D., Professor of Pediatrics and Head of the Mailman Center for Child Development, University of Miami School of Medicine, provided a preliminary appraisal of the new and developing research.

It appeared that interim developments were indeed significant. Investigators working in the field have identified a number of new areas where touch comes into play in facilitating the health and well-being of the individual, beginning before birth and continuing throughout life. Research conducted with animals and among babies in many cultures has shown dramatic physiological and emotional differences between those who have received touch and those who have not. On the basis of the findings, Johnson & Johnson felt it highly appropriate to convene a new Pediatric Round Table on the subject.

In the spring of 1989, Dr. Field, together with Dr. T. Berry Brazelton, internationally renowned Harvard Medical School authority on child development and a leading pediatrician, served as moderators for Pediatric Round Table #14, "Update on Touch." Along with a multidisciplinary faculty of seventeen specialists, they focused on bringing together important new research on the role and power of touch and discussing its implications in human development.

Advances in Touch thus offers state-of-the-art scientific information on touch, for the benefit of health care providers and the public at large — especially for parents, who need the knowledge most of all. Johnson & Johnson is proud to be associated with this endeavor and most appreciative that a faculty of such caliber could be drawn together to contribute to it.

James T. Dettre
Consultant, Marketing Communications

Robert B. Rock, Jr.
Consultant, Professional Relations

INTRODUCTION

Touch provides many different functions for all humans. For the human infant, touch has many adaptive aspects. We focus here on the infant as an illustration of the critical significance of touch.

In the uterus, the walls of the womb provide containment for the fetus and give the fetus an opportunity to start developing and learning. Within this tactile environment, the fetus can respond in safe and important ways to stimuli from the outside world. Late in gestation, the fetus can be stimulated with auditory and visual stimuli. At that time, we begin to see adaptive responses and evidence for early learning.

An example can be found in work with seven-month fetuses in which ultrasound is used to visualize their behavior. When a buzzer is sounded about 18 inches from the mother's abdomen, the whole fetus jumps with the first buzzer, but by the fourth buzzer there is no movement at all, and by the fifth buzzer the fetus starts sucking. The fetus closes her eyes and turns away from the buzzer. Then, if we use a soft rattle next to the abdomen, the fetus takes her thumb out of her mouth, opens her eyes, and looks in the direction of the rattle. She is differentiating between positive and negative stimuli within the safety of the containing uterus. The same sequence can be seen when a bright operating-room light is used as the stimulus. The first light causes a startle, but by the fourth time the fetus again closes her eyes and turns away. If a pinpoint light is then placed on the mother's abdomen, she will take her thumb out of her mouth and look in the direction of the light on the abdomen. She has habituated to the negative stimulus and alerted to the positive one. She even uses hand-to-mouth activity as a way of organizing herself. The whole fetus becomes available to what could be called learning. Thus, the baby seems to be enclosed in a safe envelope that organizes her activities.

Touch provides the baby with an adaptive and containing opportunity by helping him handle sensory and motor overload. Differentiating between positive and negative stimuli and habituating to stimuli can begin in the uterus the job of mastering responses to stimulation. Autonomic and central nervous system development begin before birth; touch and containment are at the base of the learning that accompanies their development.

After birth, parents provide this containing touch for security and add to it a soothing and a stimulating, alerting touch. They use different forms of touch as the language of communication and of attachment. Over time, the important job of learning about secure dependence comes to be mediated in large part by touch. Parent and infant learn about each other through tactile channels. Holding, containing, stroking, and lightly touching to alert are all forms of attachment. When the touch is appropriate to the baby and to his mood, it becomes a source of positive learning. When it is inappropriate — intrusive or overwhelming — it can become a source of negative learning. Even the possibility of learning to fail can result from continuous inappropriate input from the environment.

It is important for us to differentiate, if we can, between appropriate touch (appropriate to that organism) and inappropriate touch. If we, as observers, attempt to do that, we need to control for certain variables. First, we must control for the baby's state, because a particular kind of touch is appropriate to certain states of consciousness and not to others. We should control for immediate past experience as well as long-term past experience with both the quality of touch and its significance to the recipient. And then, by using what we know of infant behavior, we can tell whether the incorporation of this stimulus has been a positive or negative experience. When parents mediate messages to infants by touch, another distinction becomes important, the difference between deprivation and violation of expectancy. Deprivation seems to come from one set of conditions — a lack of stimuli — but violation of a learned expectancy is even more devastating to the organization of the infant than lack of experience. There is an enormous range of stimulation that must be judged, from the best down through deprivation and finally to violation. Violation of expectancy or violation of opportunity is more than just lack of stimulation; it can lead to disruption of the organization available in the baby. Touch must be judged with these qualities in mind.

As infants develop in the parent-infant system, they can learn to fail just as easily as they learn to succeed. Within the model of early learning, there is always an opportunity to learn to fail or to learn to succeed. A baby can learn to fail from an environment that is not nurturing, that does not touch or contain in a way that is appropriate to that baby. It is important to find out from behavioral observation whether or not the infant feels successful and if not, whether that comes from the baby's inability to organize stimuli or from the parents' or caregivers' insensitivity in conveying information.

The papers in this volume begin to look at the quality and meaning of touch and its subtleties. For example, touch may bring with it power as well as opportunities for attachment, and these messages are conveyed unconsciously by parents. They may be conveyed differently to the two genders. Cross-cultural work gives us a window into touch as it is used around the world. The different ways of holding, carrying, and touching that have evolved over many generations give us an opportunity to observe what it means to the infant, to the parents, and to the culture.

The Japanese distinguish four layers of what they call *kizuna*, or attachment: attachment from parent to baby and vice versa, from baby and parent to extended family, from baby and parent to extended family and then to the culture, and finally from baby and parent in an extended family and culture to religion. All four layers are represented in the Japanese use of carrying, swaddling, handling, touch, and massage. It seems critical, if we are looking at a system as important as touch and the communications that it carries with it, to embed our observations in these four layers in our own culture.

All the papers in this volume can lead us to use our knowledge toward national emergencies or real threats to our society such as malnutrition and cocaine addiction — problems that are handed on from parents to their babies. Those babies need extra containment, such as swaddling, that provides safety for their fragility. They are overwhelmed by sensory stimuli. Their opportunity to learn about themselves and their environment may be significantly delayed after delivery. How do we help these babies enter a nurturing world? Can we use touch to help them adapt? How do we give these babies a decent chance for future central nervous system and autonomic organization? This Round Table and this volume come at a very critical time in our history when we need to consider models for coping with crises in the next several years. The proper use of touch may make the difference in a decent recovery and outcome for large groups of high-risk infants such as these.

In the last decade significant advances have been made in the science and art of touching. Just as scientists have begun to understand the evolutionary significance and biological mechanisms underlying touch, society is beginning to realize the importance of touch for human development and social interaction. Because the science and practice of touch spans the development of several species and many cultures, touch can be better understood in those contexts. The NOVA film *The Sensitivity of Touch* and the first Johnson & Johnson Pediatric Round Table publication on touch, *The Many Facets of*

Touch (1984) stimulated significant growth in this research field. It was for that reason that we convened a second Pediatric Round Table on the subject of touch ("Update on Touch"), which is briefly summarized in this volume.

In an evolutionary and developmental progression, Pediatric Round Table #14 covered data from animal models (the rat and the monkey) to human data on the significance of touch from the time of birth until the time of death. From the rat model we learned that touch is critical for growth; without it, growth hormone levels decrease and growth is stunted (Schanberg et al.). Brain chemicals called beta-endorphins appear to be the primary mediator of this process. To reinstate growth in the maternal-touch-deprived rat pup, the mother's tongue-licking must be simulated, as by brushing the pup's skin with a wet paintbrush. Similarly, learning and memory are impaired in touch-deprived rats (Meaney et al.). Older rats who were not handled as infants show less development in the hippocampal area of the brain and memory losses that may be a model for senility in the aging human. Monkey data on touch and the immune system suggest that early tactile stimulation is critical for the development of the immune system (Reite). Touch experiences are fundamental to the establishment of attachment bonds that are thought to promote regulation of physiological — including immunological — systems.

Understanding the significance of touch for the human comes, in part, from cross-cultural comparisons. In contrast to our Western society, cultures such as the Efe pygmies, a foraging people living in the Ituri Forest of Zaire, hold their infants and young children virtually 100 percent of the time (Tronick, Winn, & Morelli). Similarly, extensive touch was seen in a slightly different life-style, in the child-rearing and extensive massaging practices of a South India fishing village (Landers).

That touch has a significant impact even before birth can be seen in research on the *doula*, a woman who rubs, strokes, and holds the pregnant woman during labor and delivery (Kennell). Observed in both Guatemalan and American deliveries, the effects of the doula's treatment are shorter labor and reduced delivery medication and anesthesia, as well as a lower rate of cesarean section and fewer perinatal complications. Following the birth, both mothers and babies were more alert and interactive. Fathers are a good substitute, and the importance of skin-to-skin contact with the newborn immediately after birth for both mothers and fathers is evidenced by their behaviors and parenting satisfaction a month after the birth (Gewirtz &

Hollenbeck).

Even more critical, perhaps, is touch for the special-needs infants and children. Premature infants are more responsive to sensitive "tender loving touch" (Tribotti) than they are to aversive routine touch of healing procedures (Healy). If they are gently massaged, they grow faster and are discharged earlier as more socially responsive babies (Field & Schanberg). Infant massage and other forms of tactile stimulation have benefits for a wide variety of infants with special needs in addition to those for normal, healthy children (Evans), and touching/carrying prevent and alleviate physiological and temperamental problems that try our parenting tolerance, such as colic and undue fussiness (Barr).

The therapeutic value of touch does not stop with infancy. Special-needs children such as deaf children and adolescent psychiatry patients are noted to benefit from touch in very different ways. For the deaf child the intact sense of touch can be used as a substitute for the damaged sense of hearing (Oller). Special devices called *tactual vocoders* transmit sound to the skin of the deaf child, presenting patterns of tactile stimulation that correspond to particular sounds. Child and adolescent psychiatric patients, who are typically not touched during hospitalization, are also noted to benefit from touch. Following massage they are less anxious (lower heart rate and cortisol levels) and happier (Larson & Field). Simple touch is also noted to reduce anxiety and postoperative pain levels in hospitalized adult and elderly patients (Heidt; Fisher & Gallant).

Thus, increasing evidence substantiates the significance of touch for the development of the body and brain and for continuing physical and mental health. Animal and, now, human data from different cultures and clinical situations make that clear. Why, then, have we developed into a relatively touch-free culture where men are more distressed than women by being touched (Fisher & Gallant; Major) and where the value of touch is largely disregarded in medical education (Older)? As one begins to identify the many uses of touch for communication and the transmission of important affect, it seems apparent that Round Tables such as this are timely and long overdue in our society. As the science and art of touch develop, so will its social acceptance and practice.

T. Berry Brazelton, M.D.,
and Tiffany M. Field, Ph.D.

PART I
ANIMAL STUDIES

MATERNAL DEPRIVATION
AND GROWTH SUPPRESSION

Saul M. Schanberg, M.D.,
Cynthia M. Kuhn, Ph.D.,
Tiffany M. Field, Ph.D.
and Jorge V. Bartolome, Ph.D.

Development in mammals is profoundly affected by environmental stimuli, and the physical stimuli provided by the mother appear to be most critical for growth and survival. Studies in our laboratory have demonstrated that even short-term interruption of mother-pup interaction in rats markedly affects several biochemical processes in the developing pup, including (1) a reduction in ornithine decarboxylase (ODC) activity, a sensitive index of cell growth and differentiation; (2) a reduction in growth hormone release; (3) an increase in the secretion of corticosterone; and (4) a suppression of tissue ODC responsivity to administered growth hormone (Schanberg & Field, 1988). The effects, which occur only during the first 18 to 20 days postnatal, are not related to changes in nutrition or temperature regulation but to the lack of active stimulation of the pup by the mother, and they can be prevented or reversed by tactile stimulation in the form of firm stroking at a specific frequency. Correlating with the animal studies, we have demonstrated that supplemental tactile stimulation facilitates weight gain and maturation of preterm neonates (Field et al., 1986) and nonorganic failure-to-thrive infants (Goldstein & Field, 1985).

There is considerable evidence that endogenous opioid neuro-peptides and receptors have an important role in development, particularly in regulation of brain maturation, both in the fetus and in the neonate. We have recently demonstrated that injecting beta-endorphin directly into the brain of newborn rat pups produces effects that mimic the effects of maternal deprivation. These studies strongly suggest that beta-endorphin or a like substance in the central nervous system could be the prime mediator of the physiological pattern of response seen following interruption of mother-pup interactions and could therefore play an important role in the regulation of tissue growth and function in the developing animal, as well as in the survival of the organism during separation.

The "Now" Enzyme

Ornithine decarboxylase is the first enzyme produced in the synthesis of the polyamines putrescine, spermine, and spermidine. These amines appear to be prime controllers of the growth and differentiation of cells, from the paramecium and tetrahymena to every type of cell in the human body. If any cell is stimulated to make more protein—if, for example, the heart is beating faster and has to synthesize more protein—ODC rises sharply.

ODC is unique in the shortness of its biological half-life: when it is made, it is destroyed very rapidly—within 10 to 20 minutes, depending on which body tissue is being tested. We call it the "now" enzyme. Because of its short life, it can serve as an index of environmental effects on biochemical and physiological processes in the developing animal; just as a muscle twitch indicates that a muscle has been stimulated, the level of ODC can tell us whether or not a cell has been stimulated.

ODC and Maternal Deprivation in Rat Pups

When rat pups are separated from the mother, the ODC enzyme

drops rapidly in every tissue of the body that we have examined, including the heart, lung, liver, kidney, spleen, and all regions of the brain. Even when the pup is placed in a temperature- and humidity-controlled environment, ODC drops within an hour and stays down as long as the separation continues. When the pup is returned to the mother, ODC returns to normal, again within a short period of time, such as an hour, depending on the tissue. This effect of maternal deprivation on ODC level lasts for about 18 days, gradually diminishing over that time, and it disappears by about day 20 — not surprisingly, since rat pups are weaned at about 22 days and normally are then on their own in any case.

What is it about maternal deprivation that causes the drop in ODC? We soon found that food was not the answer. If we gently tied off the mother's nipples but left the pups with the mother, ODC did not drop in the pups. Pups separated from their mothers showed the drop, however, even when they received the normal caloric intake. Moreover, when the mother is anesthetized and the pups are left with her to suckle, their ODC indicated that they were in effect deprived, despite the fact that their caloric intake remained normal.

Visual, auditory, and olfactory sources of stimulation were also found not to influence ODC activity. Some of these senses do not mature until several weeks after birth, whereas the change in ODC was observable within two days after birth. Results of many different types of experiments made it appear to be the interruption in active tactile interaction between mother and pup that triggered the ODC decline. As the pups left with the anesthetized mother were able to crawl all over her and each other and yet still showed the drop in ODC, it was clear that something the mother was doing to the pups, not something the pups were doing to the mother, was key.

Several other biochemical processes were also found to be affected by the interruption of this mother-pup interaction. Corticosterone levels increased, and the release of growth hormone was reduced. Because growth hormone is known to be a regulator of ODC activity in brain and peripheral tissues (Roger, Schanberg, & Fellows, 1974), we tried reversing the drop in ODC activity by injecting pups with ovine growth hormone during separation from the mother. We found, however, that ODC activity was completely unresponsive to exogenously administered growth hormone during separation.

Parallel Observations in Human Infants

These observations showed a striking resemblance to the condition known as psychosocial dwarfism (nonorganic failure to thrive), which is thought to result from withdrawal of loving care (Casler, 1961). It too is characterized by a disruption of growth hormone release and loss of responsivity to exogenous growth hormone (Powell, Brasel, & Blizzard, 1967; Powell et al., 1967). Such children, when hospitalized for tests that revealed no physiological basis for the condition, were observed to revert to normal in their secretion of and responsivity to growth hormone under the "tender, loving care" of pediatric personnel.

Reversing ODC Decline with Touch

Having concluded that lack of maternal stimulation was the key to the effects we were observing in the rat pups when they were separated from the mother, we began to look for ways to reverse the deprivation syndrome without returning the pups to the mother. Various forms of tactile stimulation were tried. Vestibular stimulation was provided in various ways with different pieces of equipment. Passive limb movements were used for kinesthetic stimulation. We tried pinching and light, gentle stroking, all to no avail. What did work was a "heavy" stroke with a dampened paint-brush at a frequency that mimicked the heavy licking patterns of the mother. When such a stroke was used, the physiological effects of deprivation were totally reversed: growth hormone rose, ODC rose, corticosterone dropped. This heavy stroking with a paintbrush worked up until about day 15 when rat pups begin to see; at that point they appeared stressed by the paintbrush procedure, and stroking no longer reversed the effects of deprivation.

In the area of human neonatology, a number of researchers have investigated the effects of supplemental stimulation on the development of preterm, low-birthweight infants. Many have demonstrated superior growth and development of the stimulated infants, although there have been some contradictory findings, particularly in weight gain. These discrepancies may be attributable to variability within and between the samples with respect to such variables as obstetric complications, birthweight, gestational age, postnatal complications, and amount of intensive care treatment, or to the type of stimulation provided.

We recently conducted a study to investigate the underlying mechanisms for those growth and behavioral gains reported in neonates receiving extra tactile/kinesthetic stimulation (Field et al., 1986). Twenty preterm neonates entering the transitional care unit ("grower" nursery) were provided tactile/kinesthetic stimulation and were compared with a control group of equivalent gestational age, birthweight, and duration of intensive care. The treatment consisted of three 15-minute periods of stimulation during three consecutive hours per day for a 10-day period.

Clinical data such as weight gain and formula intake were recorded on a daily basis. At the end of the 10-day period, the neonates were given the Brazelton (1973) Neonatal Behavioral Assessment Scale (NBAS) and their sleep/wake behavior was monitored over a 45-minute period. Data analyses revealed:

1. The treated infants averaged 47 percent more weight gain per day than the control infants, even though the groups received the same number of feedings per day and the same average formula intake, both before and during the treatment period.

2. The treated infants were awake (in drowsy or alert inactivity) and active a greater percentage of time during the sleep/wake behavioral observations.

3. The Brazelton NBAS showed the treated infants to have more mature habituation, orientation, motor, and range of state behavior.

4. Hospitalization of the treated infants was six days shorter than that of the control infants after onset of the treatment period, yielding an average hospital cost savings of $3,000 per infant.

These data suggest that tactile/kinesthetic stimulation can benefit very small, preterm neonates experiencing maternal separation during their stay in the transitional care nursery.

The Neurochemical Mechanism

In an attempt to identify the mechanism responsible for the effects of maternal deprivation and its reversal, we looked for a pharmacological agent that would lower protein synthesis in every organ throughout the body. We found that if we injected beta-endorphin centrally into the brain of the rat pup, ODC values in every organ went down, mimicking the effect of maternal deprivation (figure 1). The result was obtained only when the beta-endorphin was administered centrally, not when it was injected subcutaneously. In the same way, central administration of beta-endorphin blocked the ability of exogenous growth hormone to stimulate ODC activity. It also is impressive that these effects are observed only during approximately the first 2.5 weeks of postnatal age.

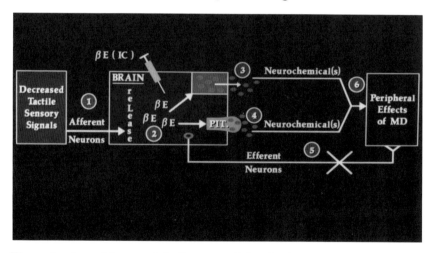

Figure 1. A working model of maternal deprivation. Deprivation lowers tactile sensory signals through afferent neurons (1), increasing the release of beta-endorphins (2), which in turn trigger the release of other neurochemicals either directly from the brain (3) or through the pituitary (4), producing the peripheral effects of maternal deprivation (MD) (6).

Similar results were obtained with centrally administered morphine. Morphine has found to be produced endogenously in the brain, along with codeine (Donnerer et al., 1986). It is possible, therefore, that morphine also plays some role along with beta-endorphin as a centrally acting intermediate in the physiological state induced by maternal deprivation.

We hypothesize that the decrease in tactile sensory signals through afferent neurons increases the release of beta-endorphin (and/or morphine), which in turn causes other neurochemicals to be released that produce the peripheral effects of maternal deprivation. These changes appear to occur through the central nervous system independent of neural pathways.

Touch and Survival

Most mammals are born totally dependent, and evolution has therefore resulted in a number of survival mechanisms designed to keep neonates and the mother together. For example, in the case of the rat mother, milk is let down for only about 45 seconds out of every 6 or 7 minutes, so that pups are kept suckling and are less inclined to wander away from the mother. The mother's licking of the pups provides another survival mechanism in providing her with replacement liquid so that she does not have to leave the nest as frequently in search of water. As the pups cannot urinate well by themselves, part of the licking pattern is a urogenital pattern in which she gets back 65 to 70 percent of the liquid she has lost from feeding the pups.

The ability of an organism to survive is also dependent on its ability to adapt to a variety of circumstances. The changes that occur in the rat pup during maternal deprivation seem to provide one such adaptation. When separated from the mother, the newborn mammal is in an acute state, having lost its major energy source. By slowing the high expenditure of energy that would normally go into the production of growth chemicals, the rat pup conserves energy for the effort of staying alive until contact between mother and pup is re-established. The process is reversed when the pup returns to the mother. The pup overreacts in many areas, avidly interacting with the mother and feeding strenuously for a time. This appears to be a time of "refueling," both physically and behaviorally.

DISCUSSION

Dr. Brazelton commented that deprivation of an expectancy that might be built into an adaptive system would be more devastating to that system than simple lack of stimulation. He wondered if the pups taken away from the mothers might not be in a violated system, not simply deprived. Failure-to-thrive babies, by contrast, have adapted to an environment in which they cannot build an expectancy that they can rely on. When they get to the hospital, where there is some consistency, even though it's minimal, they begin to build an expectancy. The expectation that the hospital routine offers physically is matched by the nurturing of the nursing staff. Tactile and holding stimuli are a vital part of this nurturance. The failing babies begin to grow and to gain weight. They begin to recover in all developmental parameters in this minimal but predictable environment. Their capacity to seek and to respond to nurturing stimuli provides a base for future caregivers. The likelihood of an improved future for these babies is enhanced. This work with rat pups, enhanced by the work with premature infants, gives us new insights into one of the parameters that contribute to such remarkable recovery.

The problems of bringing about that reversal with preterm infants were brought up. Some such neonates have so many adverse conditions that touch of any kind is at first aversive to them and may have negative consequences. Dr. Brazelton replied that we must look at the whole system, the broader underlying context of the intervention, not just what we do in a cause-and-effect relation.

NEONATAL HANDLING AND THE DEVELOPMENT OF THE ADRENOCORTICAL RESPONSE TO STRESS

Michael J. Meaney, Ph.D.,
David H. Aitken, M.Sc.,
Seema Bhatnagar, M.Sc.,
Shari R. Bodnoff, M.A.,
John B. Mitchell, Ph.D.,
and Alain Sarrieau, Ph.D.

In the early 1960s, Seymour Levine, Victor Denenberg, and their colleagues published a series of papers describing the effects of postnatal handling on the development of behavioral and endocrine responses to stress. The handling procedure involved removing rat pups from their cages, placing them in small containers, and 15 to 20 minutes later returning them to their cages and reuniting them with their mothers. This manipulation was performed once a day for the first 21 days of life. As adults, those rats that had been handled (H) exhibited less fear in novel environments and a less pronounced increase in the secretion of the adrenal glucocorticoids in response to a variety of stressors than rats that had not been handled (NH). These findings clearly demonstrated that the development of rudimentary adaptive responses to stress could be modified by environmental events.

In the studies described here, we have followed on the earlier handling studies, examining the way in which early environmental events alter the development of specific biochemical systems in the brain. We have shown how early handling influences the neurochemical development of certain brain regions that regulate the endocrine response to stress. Neonatal handling increases the efficiency of adaptive endocrine responses to stress, shielding the animal from excessive exposure to the highly catabolic adrenal steroids. In later life, this effect appears to protect the animal from potentially damaging effects of these steroids, ensuring more efficient cognitive functioning.

The Effect of Handling
on the Adrenocortical Response to Stress

The hypothalamic-pituitary-adrenal (HPA) axis is highly responsive to stress (see figure 2; Selye, 1950). During stress, the secretion of hypothalamic releasing factors, such as corticotropin-releasing factor (CRF) and vasopressin, causes an increase in the release of pituitary adrenocorticotropin (ACTH) into circulation (Antoni, 1986; Gibbs, 1986; Plotsky & Vale, 1984; Rivier & Plotsky, 1986; Rivier & Vale, 1983; Rivier et al., 1982). The increased levels of ACTH in turn result in a dramatic increase in the release of adrenal glucocorticoids, which initiate a series of reactions that help the organism cope with the stress by increasing the availability of energy substrates and suppressing immunological responses (Munck, Guyre, & Holbrook, 1984) that could interfere with needed mobility.

Continued exposure to this state of enhanced catabolism can present a serious risk to the organism, however; in addition to a general suppression of anabolic processes, prolonged glucocorticoid exposure can lead to muscle atrophy, decreased sensitivity to insulin and a risk of steroid-induced diabetes, hypertension, hyperlipidemia, hypercholesterolemia, arterial disease, amenorrhea and impotency, and the impairment of growth and tissue repair, as well as immunosuppression (see Munck, Guyre, & Holbrook, 1984). It is therefore in the animal's best interest to turn off the glucocorticoid response and return to basal glucocorticoid levels once the stress is terminated. This pituitary-adrenal response to stress is terminated by the inhibitory, or negative-feedback, actions of glucocorticoids on those brain regions that regulate the release of pituitary hormones. Briefly, the high levels of glucocorticoids achieved during stress serve to inhibit the synthesis and release of CRF, vasopressin, and other releasing factors from the hypothalamus and to dampen the responsiveness of pituitary corticotrophes, resulting in a decrease in the release of ACTH. Thus, once the excitatory signal associated with the stressor has passed, the inhibitory effects of the high glucocorticoid levels are fully exerted, and the pituitary-adrenal response is terminated (Dallman et al., 1987; Jones et al., 1982; Keller-Wood & Dallman, 1984; Plotsky, Otto, & Sapolsky, 1986; Van Loon & De Souza, 1987). In large part, these inhibitory effects are mediated by the binding of the steroid to an intracellular corticosteroid receptor, and receptor-binding capacity

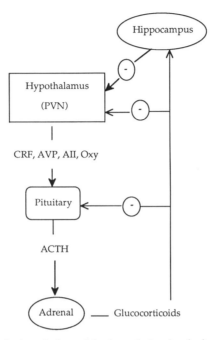

Figure 2. Schematic description of the hypothalamic-pituitary-adrenal (HPA) response to stress. In response to neural signals emanating from various sources, the hypothalamus releases corticotropin-releasing factor (CRF), vasopressin (AVP), angiotensin II (AII), and oxytocin (Oxy) into the pituitary. These hormones lead to an increase in the secretion of ACTH into circulation, stimulating glucocorticoid release from the adrenal cortex. Glucocorticoids in circulation in turn act at the level of the pituitary to dampen the response to hypothalamic releasing factors and at the level of the hypothalamus and the hippocampus to inhibit CRF release.

therefore becomes a rate-limiting step in determining the sensitivity of the cell to the glucocorticoid.

The principal glucocorticoid in the rat is corticosterone; in humans and other primates it is cortisol. Under normal, resting conditions, young adult H and NH rats do not differ in basal corticosterone levels at any time over the diurnal cycle (Meaney, Aitken, Sharma, & Viau, in press; Meaney et al., 1989). In response to a variety of stressors, however, adult animals handled in the early postnatal period secrete less corticosterone and show a faster return to basal corticosterone levels than do NH rats (Ader & Grota, 1969; Hess et al., 1969; Levine, 1957, 1962; Meaney, Aitken, Bodnoff, Iny, & Sapolsky, 1985; Meaney et al., 1989). These differences are not due to altered adrenal sensitivity to ACTH or pituitary sensitivity to CRF (Meaney et al., 1989). Nor are there differences between H and NH animals in the metabolic clearance rate for corticosterone (Meaney et al., 1989; Zarrow, Campbel, & Denenberg, 1972). Rather, the difference lies in the fact that the NH animals show increased secretion of corticosterone.

If the critical difference is located above the hypothalamic-pituitary level, then we would expect H and NH animals also to differ in ACTH and CRF responses to stress. This is indeed the case. Both during stress and following the termination of stress, levels of ACTH and CRF are higher in NH animals than in H animals (Meaney ct al., 1989). These findings suggest that the mechanism or mechanisms for the differences between H and NH animals may be related to differences in sensitivity of central nervous system (CNS) negative-feedback processes.

Glucocorticoid Receptor Systems

The activity of the HPA axis, under both basal and stressful conditions, is regulated by specific brain regions, most notably the hypothalamus, the amygdala, the septum, and the hippocampus (Dallman et al., 1987; Feldman & Conforti, 1980; Fischette et al., 1980; Sapolsky, Krey, & McEwen, 1984). Cells within these regions contain receptor proteins that bind corticosterone and convey the steroidal signal. The predominant neural receptor for corticosterone in the rat is the glucocorticoid receptor, a soluble macromolecule found in both neurons and glia (for a review, see McEwen, DeKloet, & Rostene, 1986). This receptor is widely distributed throughout the brain, with the highest concentrations in the hippocampus, cortex, hypothalamus, septum, amygdala, and several midbrain structures such as the raphe and the locus coeruleus. We have recently demonstrated the existence of a pharmacologically identical glucocorticoid receptor in human temporal cortex (Sarrieau et al., 1988).

In addition to this receptor, a second binding site for corticosterone in the brain has now been clearly identified (Beaumont & Fanestil,

1983; Krozowski & Funder, 1983; Reul & DeKloet, 1985; Reul, van den Bosch, & DeKloet, 1987). This receptor is pharmacologically identical to the mineralocorticoid receptor found in the kidney: it binds corticosterone and aldosterone with high affinity, but it binds synthetic glucocorticoids with very low affinity.

Glucocorticoids in the bloodstream inhibit ACTH release from the pituitary and CRF release from the hypothalamus (Dallman et al., 1987; Keller-Wood & Dallman, 1984; Plotsky & Vale, 1984; see figure 2). There is now considerable evidence that the hippocampus is a critical structure in the feedback process (Feldman & Conforti, 1980; Sapolsky, Krey, & McEwen, 1984, 1986). In the adult rat, hippocampal destruction causes elevated corticosterone levels under both basal, stress, and post-stress conditions. Moreover, hippocampectomized animals show reduced suppression of ACTH following exogenous glucocorticoid administration (Feldman & Conforti, 1980). These findings, together with the fact that the hippocampus is rich in receptors for corticosterone, have suggested that this structure is involved in the inhibitory influence of glucocorticoids over adrenocortical activity.

The glucocorticoid receptor system is highly responsive to stress, whereas the response of the mineralocorticoid-like receptor system to stress is minimal (Sapolsky, Krey, & McEwen, 1983a; see also Meaney, Viau, et al., 1988; Reul & DeKloet, 1985). Moreover, it is to the glucocorticoid receptors that the synthetic corticoids, which are known to have negative-feedback efficacy, selectively bind. These findings strongly suggest that the glucocorticoid receptor, and not the mineralocorticoid-like receptor, is responsible for the negative-feedback actions of the glucocorticoids at the hippocampal level.

A reduction in the number of glucocorticoid receptors in the hippocampus could therefore desensitize this structure to the glucocorticoids and thus dampen adrenocortical negative feedback. Evidence from a number of models supports this idea; in each case, a decrease in hippocampal glucocorticoid receptor-binding capacity (reflecting a decreased number of receptor sites) is associated with hypersecretion of corticosterone following the termination of the stressor, indicating less effective negative feedback. For example, the aged rat, which has an extensive loss of receptors in the hippocampus and a moderate loss in the amygdala, shows elevated corticosterone following stress far longer than the young adult animal, suggesting that adrenocortical negative feedback is less efficient in older animals (Meaney, Aitken et al., 1988; Reul, Tonnaer, & DeKloet, 1988; Ritger, Veldhuis, & DeKloet, 1984; Sapolsky, Krey, & McEwen, 1983a, 1984, 1986).

The Effect of Handling on
HPA Negative-Feedback Processes

On the basis of the relative hypersecretion of corticosterone by NH animals, we wondered whether adult H and NH animals might differ in negative-feedback sensitivity to circulating glucocorticoids. We tested this idea using a classical feedback paradigm based on the work of Dallman and her colleagues, who showed that high levels of circulating glucocorticoids inhibit subsequent hypothalamic-pituitary activity (Dallman et al., 1987; Keller-Wood & Dallman, 1984). We injected adult H and NH animals with either corticosterone or dexamethasone 3 hours prior to a 10-minute immobilization stress and found that both glucocorticoids were more effective in suppressing stress-induced HPA responses in the H animals (Meaney et al., 1989). These data suggest that indeed the H animals are more sensitive to the negative-feedback effects of circulating glucocorticoids on stress-induced HPA activity.

Because the negative-feedback process is, at least in large measure, mediated by the binding of corticosterone to intracellular receptors, we have measured both glucocorticoid and mineralocorticoid-like receptors in selected brain regions and pituitary of H and NH animals (Meaney & Aitken, 1985; Meaney, Aitken, Bodnoff, Iny, Tatarewicz, & Sapolsky, 1985; Meaney, Aitken, & Sapolsky, 1987; Meaney, Aitken, Sharma, & Viau, in press; Meaney et al., 1989; Meaney, Viau et al., 1988; Sarrieau, Sharma, & Meaney, 1988). We have found that handled animals show increased glucocorticoid receptor-binding capacity in the hippocampus, but not in the septum, amygdala, hypothalamus, or pituitary. The difference occurs in glucocorticoid but not mineralocorticoid-like receptor-binding capacity and is clearly related to the number of receptor sites. In a recent study (Meaney et al., 1989), we demonstrated that the difference in hippocampal glucocorticoid receptor-binding capacity is related to the greater negative-feedback efficiency of the H animals. Thus it appears that one critical feature of the handling effect is the permanent increase in the glucocorticoid receptor sites in the hippocampus.

In our initial studies, animals were handled during the first 21 days of life. Subsequent studies to determine whether some portion of this period represents a critical period for the handling effect demonstrated that glucocorticoid receptor-binding capacity appears to be vulnerable to environmental regulation during the first 2 weeks of life. Handling between days 1 and 7 of life was as effective in increasing hippocampal glucocorticoid receptor-binding capacity as handling over the entire first 3 weeks. Handling done only over the second week of life (between days 8 and 14) was also effective, whereas animals handled only between days 15 and 21 did not differ from NH animals in glucocorticoid receptor-binding capacity (Meaney & Aitken, 1985). This temporal pattern corresponds to the normal developmental changes in glucocorticoid receptor-binding capacity, which is low on day 3 and increases steadily, achieving adult values by about day 15.

The mechanism by which handling regulates hippocampal development, we hypothesize, is a series of events triggered by the sensory stimuli associated with the handling manipulation. Tactile stimulation leads to a mild and transient drop in the pup's body temperature (Sullivan, Wilson, & Leon, 1988). Changes in body temperature are a potent stimulus for the activation of the hypothalamic-pituitary-thyroid axis, leading to increased levels of circulating thyroxine (T_4) and intracellular levels of triiodothyronine (T_3). A study (Meaney, Aitken, & Sapolsky, 1987) exposing neonatal rat pups to these hormones suggests that the hormones may indeed mediate the effects of neonatal handling on the development of CNS receptor systems that regulate HPA activity, by increasing levels of serotonin, which has a profound effect on glucocorticoid receptor-binding capacity both in vivo and in cultured hippocampal cells (Mitchell et al., in press; Mitchell, Iny, & Meaney, in press). One critical feature of this effect, which we must ultimately account for, is that the increase in glucocorticoid receptors persists throughout the animal's life. This is probably one of the most intriguing features of this developmental effect.

The Effect of Handling on Later Brain Aging

Do the changes in HPA function occurring as a result of handling have any bearing on the animal's biological fitness? In a recent series of studies, we have been examining the brain aging process in H and

NH rats. The results of these studies clearly demonstrate that these neuroendocrine changes are of considerable importance for the animals in later life.

Recent research has shown that increased exposure to glucocorticoids in later life can result in the death of hippocampal neurons and the emergence of severe cognitive deficits. Under both basal and stressful conditions, plasma glucocorticoids in the rat increase with age (DeKosky, Scheff, & Cotman, 1984; Meaney, Aitken, Sharma, & Viau, in press; Meaney, Viau et al., 1988; Sapolsky, Krey, & McEwen, 1983b, 1986). This increased HPA activity is associated with decreased CNS negative-feedback inhibition over hypothalamic-pituitary activity, so that ACTH levels also increase with age (Meaney, Aitken, Sharma, & Viau, in press; Tang & Phillips, 1978). As the rat ages, there is a loss of receptors for corticosterone, which dampens the efficacy of negative feedback in inhibiting HPA activity, and an increase in circulating glucocorticoid levels results.

This increase in circulating corticosterone has important consequences for neuronal function. Landfield and his colleagues (Landfield et al., 1978, 1981) demonstrated that the occurrence of hippocampal neuron loss was positively correlated with the increase in HPA activity. They then adrenalectomized rats at midlife (12 months of age) and found that these animals later showed little or no evidence of hippocampal neuron loss or the spatial memory deficits that are common in later life and closely associated with hippocampal dysfunction. Young adult rats treated for 3 months with exogenous corticosterone, mimicking the elevated basal levels seen in certain old rats, show profound hippocampal loss (Sapolsky, Krey, & McEwen, 1985). Finally, 24- to 26-month-old rats who were identified as cognitively age-impaired were found to have increased HPA function under both basal and stressful conditions, whereas aged animals who were not impaired did not differ from 6-month-old controls in HPA activity (Issa, Rowe, Gauthier, & Meaney, submitted). Taken together, these data strongly suggest that increased glucocorticoid exposure is associated with the occurrence of neuropathology and impaired cognition in later life.

Considering the more efficient negative-feedback inhibition over HPA function in the rats that had been handled, we wondered whether these animals might be "protected" from glucocorticoid-induced hippocampal neuropathology in later life. In the studies designed to examine this question, we have compared H and NH animals 6 to 26 months of age. The results of the studies suggest that neonatal handling has remarkable consequences for the animal in later life.

Throughout life, H animals have a significantly higher number of hippocampal glucocorticoid receptors than do NH animals (Meaney, Aitken et al., 1988; Meaney, Aitken, Bhatnagar, & Sapolsky, in press; Meaney, Aitken, Sharma, & Viau, in press). As expected, we found that the age-related HPA deficits were far less pronounced in the H rats (Meaney, Aitken, Bhatnagar, & Sapolsky, in press; Meaney, Aitken et al., 1988). These animals secreted less corticosterone during immobilization stress, and following stress they terminated corticosterone secretion sooner than did the NH rats. Moreover, the age-related rise in basal corticosterone levels, typically seen in aged rats, was observed in the NH but not in the H animals.

These findings suggested that cumulative exposure to the highly catabolic glucocorticoids over the lifespan was greater in the NH animals and that the expected hippocampal degeneration would be less pronounced in the H animals. This is exactly what we observed. Among NH animals but not H animals, there occurred a significant loss of hippocampal neurons. Importantly, H and NH rats did not differ in number of cells at six months of age; rather, handling attenuated the loss of hippocampal neurons occurring at later ages.

This difference in hippocampal cell number between the older H and NH animals was of functional significance. The hippocampus is of considerable importance in learning and memory, and hippocampal injury profoundly disrupts cognition (see Morris et al., 1982). These facts suggest that the older H rats should show less evidence of age-related cognitive impairments than older NH rats. In fact, in experiments designed to test spatial memory, 24-month-old H animals performed as well as 6-month-old animals, whereas the older NH rats performed significantly less well than younger animals (Meaney, Aitken, Bhatnagar, & Sapolsky, in press; Meaney, Aitken et al., 1988).

The diminished rate of hippocampal neuron loss in the aging H rats probably reflects the lower cumulative lifetime exposure to glucocorticoids. It should be noted that this outcome is the product of two apparently opposing trends. While the increased concentrations of hippocampal glucocorticoid receptors are related to the enhanced negative-feedback sensitivity and decreased glucocorticoid secretion in the H rats, the same high glucocorticoid receptor concentrations could conceivably sensitize the hippocampus to the endangering effects of glucocorticoids. In this instance, the decreased secretion apparently outweighs the risk of increased target sensitivity, perhaps by ensuring that the prolonged glucocorticoid exposure necessary for the endangering effects does not occur.

Thus, an environmental manipulation occurring early in life results in a sequence of changes that endure throughout the lifespan, with dramatic attenuation of some of the deficits typical of aging. These findings cast considerable light upon the regulatory relationships linking adrenocortical secretory patterns, hippocampal glucocorticoid receptor concentrations, and hippocampal pathology and dysfunction. In addition, they demonstrate that relatively subtle individual differences in early experience can profoundly alter the quality of aging years later. They underscore the importance of developmental critical periods and explain a possible source of variability in aging studies. It is important that H and NH animals do not differ in hippocampal neuron number and spatial memory at six months of age; rather, the difference emerges over time as the function of an interaction with age. Thus, the H/NH differences in these measures at later ages represent a true retardation of the aging process in the H rats.

DISCUSSION

Dr. Barr asked for clarification of Dr. Meaney's interpretation of the handling maneuver. Is it a positive or negative action, and what is it about the handling that has the effects that have been observed? Dr. Meaney replied that it is hard to determine the critical components of the manipulation, because the stress response in the neonate is so different from that in the adult. He and his colleagues have been thinking of it as providing a certain amount of environmental stimulation.

Dr. Meaney then added that "a little light bulb" had gone off during Dr. Schanberg's talk. To be effective, the handling must involve the pup; handling only the mother has no effect. But handling the pups alters the mother/infant interactions. Normally these interactions follow a stereotypical pattern of feeding periods of 25 to 30 minutes, during which time the mother's body temperature increases, followed by periods of about 20 minutes when she gets off her pups and body temperature dissipates. When the animals are handled, the overall amount of time the mother is on the pups does not change, but the nesting periods become considerably shorter; the mother gets on and off the nest more frequently. When the mother gets on the nest, she draws the pups underneath her and stimulates them tactilely with urogenital licking. It has been suggested that this form of stimulation is important to early development. It is possible that providing a short disruption induces more mother/infant interaction that is mediated biologically with mechanisms having to do with feeding.

Dr. Kennell wondered whether any data existed on the effects on humans of ACTH and corticosteroids administered in early life. Dr. Meaney replied that computer-assisted tomography has produced evidence of reversible cerebral atrophies associated with glucocorticoid and ACTH therapies. Exposure to glucocorticoids and ACTH is also associated with changes in metabolism. There is clear evidence going back to the early 1950s that persistent exposure to elevated corticoids results in reversible cognitive deficits; it is seen in depressive patients who hypersecrete cortisone. Research is currently underway in his laboratory on two populations in later life: depressed patients who hypersecrete cortisol and arthritic and asthmatic patients who have been exposed to glucocorticoid therapy for long periods of time. Dr. Kennell suggested that another population that might be studied is the large group of premature infants with retrolental fibroplasia who were treated with glucocorticoids many years ago.

Dr. Schanberg pointed out that conditions in the laboratory are not the same as conditions in the wild, and the normal, natural hormonal state of an animal in the wild is probably what is best for that animal at that stage of its development. "Evolution's been at work a very long time," he noted. He doubted that artificially raising or lowering hormonal levels ever benefited the development of a rat or any other animal. He concluded, "I think that every time we start to think that we are going to manipulate hormones or something else early on and come out with something better, we're going to lose."

The differences between laboratory conditions and the natural state also interested Dr. Brazelton, who pointed out that in the wild the separations of mother and pups would be more frightening and the reunions would be more critical and adaptive. At what point, he wondered, would the model of learning from stress become a negative learning model instead of a positive one? Dr. Meaney noted that his research, while not naturalistic in removing the pups from the nest, had been within the natural time frame of maternal separations and returns. Seymour Levine has been working with longer periods of maternal deprivation, and early data suggest that the effects are very different from those of the handling experiments.

Dr. Tronick wondered what effects the handling had on the behavior of the pups themselves. In normal interactions, stress and recovery from stress result in changes in coping and regulatory behaviors that are positive, but if stress becomes chronic, patterns are disrupted and coping mechanisms that are effective for acute stresses — for example, withdrawal — become chronic, and development is compromised. The speeded-up periods when the mother gets off the pups must result in modification of their hormonal and biological systems and doubtless of their behavioral systems as well. Dr. Meaney replied that physiologically they showed differences in terms of their endocrine regulation and body temperature.

EFFECTS OF TOUCH ON THE IMMUNE SYSTEM*

Martin Reite, M.D.

There is substantial evidence suggesting that touch is involved in immune system function, although it is likely that the relationships are indirect. This paper reviews several relevant facets of such a possible relationship: (1) the skin as an immunologic and immunoresponsive

*ACKNOWLEDGMENTS This manuscript was prepared while the author was a Fellow at the Center for Advanced Study in the Behavioral Sciences. Grateful acknowledgment is made for financial support provided by the John D. & Catherine T. MacArthur Foundation and by USPHS Research Scientist Award #MH46335.

organ; (2) direct effects of skin stimulation (touch) on immunological function; and (3) indirect, including symbolic, effects of touch on immune measures.

Immunity and the Immune System

Immunity refers to all mechanisms used by the body as protection against environmental agents foreign to the body. The immune system consists of two divisions, *innate immunity* and *acquired immunity.*

Innate immunity refers to those immune mechanisms that the organism is born with. It includes physical barriers such as the skin and mucous membranes, chemical barriers such as the acidity of sweat, and the cellular activities of leukocytes, phagocytic monocytes, and eosinophils.

Acquired immunity, unlike innate immunity, is specific to particular invaders and usually results from prior contact with an invader. It has a cellular component and a humoral component. Cellular immunity is mediated by several types of cells found in the blood and lymphatic system, including polymorphonuclear leukocytes, eosinophils, and macrophages. Humoral immunity is mediated by serum antibodies, which are a mixture of serum globulins called *immunoglobulins.*

The immune system is complex, with multiple components. Measuring its function is therefore also complex and can be problematic; exactly what is being measured must be carefully evaluated. One frequently reported procedure measures the degree to which lymphocytes isolated from a blood sample proliferate and differentiate in vitro in response to a mitogen, a substance known to promote their growth and division. A single blood sample may provide a biased sample of lymphocytes (Butcher, 1986; Cohen & Crnic, 1984; Maier & Laudenslager, 1988), however, and in any case the clinical significance of this measure is not clear. Another assessment technique involves injecting a foreign antigen and measuring the timing and amount of the antibody response. This procedure tests components of both the cellular and the humoral systems, but it is somewhat complex to perform and involves immunization with a foreign protein. Injecting an antigen into the skin and measuring the hypersensitivity response is perhaps a better overall test of immune system function.

Regulation of the immune system is equally complex. There is evidence that the central nervous system (CNS) may have direct communication with portions of the immune system (Felten et al., 1985; Felten et al., 1987; Livnat et al., 1985). If so, anything that alters CNS function may also have a potential effect on immune system function. Similarly, a close relationship has been found between a variety of neuroendocrine measures and the immune system (Smith & Blalock, 1988). Behavioral influences on immune system function have also been identified, although they are still not well understood. Sleep appears to be closely related to immunological function (Moldofsky et al., 1986; Reite et al., 1987), as are circadian rhythms (Cohen & Crnic, 1982). Finally, immune function may be affected by nutritional factors (Beisel et al., 1981; Chandra, 1983) and by stressful experiences that activate the pituitary-adrenal system (Cohen & Crnic, 1982). Moreover, it is possible to condition aspects of immune system function (Irwin & Livnat, 1987), so that some aspects of immunological functioning may be modulated by learning.

The Skin as an Immunologic and Immunoresponsive Organ

The role of the skin in expressing immune responses has long been known. Dermatitis is a frequent symptom of allergic disorders, and many more serious immunopathies have substantial symptoms seen in the skin. More recent evidence suggests that the skin, specifically the epidermis, may itself be an active component of the immune system, playing several roles in cellular immunity (Chu et al., 1983; Rubenfeld et al., 1981; Sauder, 1983; Streilein, 1983).

Skin Stimulation (Touch) and Immunological Function

Studies that purport to examine the effects of touch on the immune function are complicated by the fact that in an environment that includes gravity we can alter touch stimulation but we cannot remove it. We can only study changes in the type or amount of touch and attempt to infer from these whether touch per se may be involved in producing the results we find.

In the early studies of rat pups that had been handled (see Meaney, this volume), handled animals were found to produce consistently higher levels of antibodies in response to injection with an antigen than nonhandled animals (Solomon, Levine, & Kraft, 1968). Subsequent studies suggested that the early handling experience was modulating the development of the adrenocortical stress-response hormone system and that this system in turn was modulating immune function.

One way in which touch experiences might influence the function of the immune system is via modulation of arousal and associated CNS/hormonal activity. Such an effect has been postulated to occur in therapeutic deep pressure touch (Krauss, 1987). In one case study (Boccia, Reite, & Laudenslager, 1989) social grooming among pigtail macaque monkeys was associated with a significant decrease in heart rate, compatible with a decrease in sympathetic nervous system activity.

Evidence from Separation Studies

Separation studies among nonhuman primates, which include marked alteration of touch stimulation, have been a useful means of studying modifications of immunological activity. When pigtail monkey infants living in a social group are separated from their mothers, they exhibit a two-stage reaction called agitation-depression or protest-despair (Kaufman & Rosenblum, 1969). When the mother is removed from the social group, the infant first experiences a period of increased activity, searching behavior, and a distress vocalization, accompanied by an activated EEG pattern and marked elevations in both heart rate and body temperature (Reite et al., 1978). Within a day or so, a depression or despair reaction emerges, characterized by decreased activity and social play behavior and development of a slouched posture and sad facial expression. The depressive reaction is accompanied by a constellation of physiological reactions, including decreases in heart rate and nocturnal body temperature (Reite et al., 1981), a slight phase delay in heart rate and body temperature circadian rhythms (Reite et al., 1982), and sleep disturbances (Reite & Short, 1978).

Similar behavioral reactions are found in many other species of monkeys, and while physiological measurements have not been performed in most studies, we might infer some similarity. In general the magnitude of the behavioral response to separation is greatest in those species in which infants are not adopted by other females in the group after the mother has been removed. There is evidence suggesting that separation experiences result in altered immune function. In several studies (Laudenslager, Reite, & Harbeck, 1982; Reite, Harbeck, & Hoffman, 1981) lymphocyte responsiveness to mitogen stimulation was suppressed during separation, recovering to baseline values following reunion. In another study (Laudenslager, Reite, & Held, 1986) monkey infants separated from their mothers demonstrated less antibody production in response to an initial injection of an antigen, although the two groups produced similar antibody levels in response to a second injection of the antigen. Altered natural killer cell activity may accompany maternal separation in young pigtail monkeys, although the direction of the response is variable (Laudenslager, 1988). Finally, evidence of a possible long-term effect of early separation experiences on later immune function was found in a study of adult pigtail monkeys who as infants had experienced a 10-day separation from mother and who now exhibited evidence of decreased lymphocyte response to mitogen stimulation (Laudenslager, Capitanio, & Reite, 1985).

What, then, mediates the immunological effects of separation? Does the stress of separation per se elevate serum cortisol, which is a potent immunosuppressor, to result in altered immune function? Studies with different species of monkeys with varying serum cortisol values and pituitary-adrenal reactivity (Coe et al., 1988; Coe, Rosenberg, & Levine, 1988; Gunnar et al., 1981; Mendoza et al., 1978; Smotherman et al., 1979) suggest that stress-induced activation of the pituitary-adrenal system alone does not account for the immunological changes observed and that other mechanisms are likely to play a significant role.

Moreover, while the loss of touch can be interpreted as one important variable in separation studies, several studies have demonstrated the importance of other variables in modulating aspects of the separation response. Infant squirrel monkeys, which showed increases in serum cortisol in response to separation from their mothers, did not demonstrate such increases when separated from cloth surrogate mothers on which they had been raised (Hennessy et al., 1979), although they exhibited behavioral distress in the form of vocalization. Conversely, infants separated from their mothers in social groups where they were adopted by other adult females exhibited relatively little behavioral distress but nonetheless showed increases in serum cortisol (Coe et al., 1978). Aunting per se, which included physical contact, did not prevent a cortisol response, whereas loss of physical contact in surrogate separation did not induce a cortisol response. In a related study of the capacity of infant squirrel monkeys to mount an antibody response to viral challenge (Coe et al., 1987), infants separated from their mothers were evaluated in several social and physical environments. Here, an unfamiliar environment appeared to be the critical variable.

Thus absence of touch is one, but only one, component of the separation experience, and factors other than touch appear to exert substantial influence over the response to separation. Related studies suggest that touch per se may not be as important as who is providing the touch experience.

Touch and Attachment

Touch experiences are fundamental to the establishment of attachment bonds, which are thought to promote regulation of physiological, possibly including immunological, systems (Reite, 1984; Reite & Capitanio, 1985). Several studies suggest that touch experiences may act in this indirect manner to activate or modulate immunological function.

In a recent study (Reite, Kaemingk, & Boccia, 1989), we recorded physiology and behavior in five bonnet monkey infants who were separated from their mothers but remained in their natal social groups. Bonnet monkeys living in social groups are quite different from pigtail monkeys; bonnet mothers tend to share their infants and there is prominent aunting behavior, so that infants spend a great deal of time with, and develop relationships with, adult females other than their own mothers (Rosenblum & Kaufman, 1967). In this study, the five infants evidenced behavioral agitation immediately following separation, but in general both the behavioral and physiological responses to separation, while similar in form, were relatively less pronounced in the bonnet infants. We believe that these findings were attributable to the fact that all five infants were adopted by other adult females in the group, generally one particular female.

Adoption alone is not sufficient to prevent substantive responses to mother loss, however. In two cases when infant monkeys, one pigtail and one bonnet, were adopted by pigtail females with whom they were familiar but with whom they had had no close physical contact, the adoption and close bodily contact did not ameliorate the effects of maternal separation (Reite, 1985; Reite, Seiler, & Short, 1978). These cases suggest that adoption per se, and the tactile stimulation it provides, is of limited or no value if there has been no previous relationship with the adoptive female.

Interestingly, a recent study (Brown et al., 1986) examined the role of social support in influencing the risk of stress-induced depression in a sample of 400 working-class women in Great Britain. Support from a "core" relationship at the time of the stress was associated with a decreased risk for depressive symptoms, but the presence of crisis support from a "non-core" relationship was not helpful and was in fact associated with a higher rate of depressive symptoms. These findings are consistent with the hypothesis that a pre-existing special relationship, perhaps an "attachment-bond," is a prerequisite for social support to have substantial benefit in modifying or buffering the response to stress.

Might these findings apply to touch as well? That is, touch provided in the context of an attachment relationship may be quite different from touch provided in another context, and who provides it may be a critical variable.

In a recent study (Boccia, Laudenslager, & Reite, 1988), restricted access to food was used to change the normally cohesive behavior of a social group of bonnet monkeys; aggression increased, a dominance hierarchy was established, submissive behaviors increased, play among infants decreased, and social grooming decreased. When the mothers of two infants raised in these conditions were removed, the efforts of other group members to adopt the infants were unsuccessful and the infants became behaviorally depressed (Boccia, Laudenslager, & Reite, unpublished). These observations support the premise that modification of early social experience, with resultant changes in social relationships, may alter the type of social support that can be provided at times of stress and so significantly alter the response to stress.

Conclusions

Evidence supporting a direct link between touch and altered immune function has yet to be developed, but it seems likely that touch may influence immune function via alterations in activity of the sympathetic nervous system. There also appears to be a close relationship between touch and social attachment, or social bonding, and in turn a close relationship between attachment and physiological, including possibly immunological, regulation. Thus the clear relationships between touch and immune function are probably mediated via the autonomic nervous system and attachment bridges.

DISCUSSION

Dr. Brazelton wondered how much the adoption behavior among monkeys living in social groups is mediated by the mother's permission to let other females handle her baby and how much comes from the baby's active soliciting and giving clear cues to other females, to get back what he needs. Dr. Reite replied that both mechanisms are clearly important. There are certainly individual differences among infants, in their rate of development and the amount of time they stay with their mothers at different ages. There is evidence of an association between certain physiological changes and time spent on the mother; infants with better developed EEGs at an early age and better developed alpha, for example, seem to be off the mother sooner, more active, and more outgoing, than infants with slower, less well-organized alpha activity, who are protected longer by the mother. In addition to these infant-relative variables, there are mother-relative variables. These were seen in the paradigm where the stress level of the bonnet group was changed through changes in the feeding patterns; the mothers became more protective of their infants and no longer permitted them to get involved with other members of the group. In this case, the variable appeared to be affected by the mother's degree of dominance in the group; the infant of the dominant female developed relationships with other females, but the infant of the most submissive female had no relationships with others. This infant was more severely impacted by the maternal separation than the infant of the dominant female.

Dr. Older drew an analogy between the two different monkey species and two ethnic groups in New Zealand, where he had first read the bonnet and pigtail monkey studies. Although he acknowledged the difficulties in associating bonnet monkeys with Maoris and pigtail monkeys with Pakeha or white New Zealanders, he noted that like the bonnets, Maoris are a very cooperative, group-oriented society. Babies are routinely shared, and adoption is handled in exactly the same way as with the bonnets. Pakeha New Zealanders are more like the pigtails — competitive, isolated, depressed when separated. Dr. Reite agreed that while it is hard to say what is homologous among the two species, they have a lot in common. The value of the animal data, he noted, is to allow us to build testable hypotheses with which to look at human populations. We can model many human cultural differences in primate populations and come up with a set of variables that we can then direct to human studies.

The importance of the role of touch in attachment was stressed by Dr. Field. Touch may be just one component of attachment, but it is the only modality that is not involved in all relationships, she pointed out. Dr. Brazelton wondered whether the role of touch in differentiating the mother from other females in the group had been studied in the separation experiments with bonnet monkeys. Dr. Reite responded that it had not, but that it would be useful to set up an experiment that looked carefully at the evolution of the relationships between the infant and other individuals in the group with respect to such things as the amount and nature of tactile contact.

Dr. Gewirtz brought up the issue of whether touch or other response is contingent on initiation. Are bonnet peers and parents more contingent than pigtails in their responding to human behavior? he asked. Such a behavioral mechanism might differentiate the species and might be a focal point for research. Dr. Reite replied that there are no data in that area. All kinds of elaborate social interactions are going on that have not yet been studied, he observed. Sometimes a pigtail infant that has been separated will reject a female who is chasing him around, trying to adopt him; other infants will chase the females, trying to be adopted, but the females will ignore them.

Dr. Meaney queried whether play partners had a role in alleviating some of the stress associated with separation. Dr. Reite reported that peers remaining in the group have an important effect in reducing the magnitude of the heart rate response. Often the separated infants will turn to the peers, staying with them and sleeping next to them. Not every research group of animals is large enough to include peers, but when there are peers, peer relationships seem to become stronger. Of course, the fact of whether or not peers are present is a source of variance in the data.

Asked whether the emotional content of the separation response is one of fear or anger, Dr. Reite replied that in the delayed, depressive component it is closest to a model of grief. In the initial reaction it is probably anxiety, closely analogous to separation anxiety in children. Anger is not necessarily involved, but fear is certainly a component, although the response is more than fear. Ms. Evans commented that the body posture and withdrawal seen in photographs of separated monkey infants are the same as the grief response seen in abused babies, orphans, and also adopted babies.

The question of whether infants become habituated to repeated separations was then discussed. No such studies that monitored physiology have been done, but Stephen Suomi has studied infants raised solely with peers, separating them and reuniting them repeatedly. He found evidence of what he thought was developmental maturational lag in the repeatedly separated animals. Dr. Field, however, reported that human preschoolers whose parents made frequent trips got used to the repeated separations. Peers are real buffers here, she noted. Dr. Brazelton added that the ambivalence of the parent about leaving the child is a critical part of the experience that needs to be taken into account.

Ms. Tribotti pointed out that the separation response is a problem too little addressed in the case of infants who have spent considerable time in intensive care nurseries and are transferred to other facilities. Such infants sometimes become profoundly depressed. How can we deal with these babies? she asked. What kind of support can we give them? These are critically important questions that remain to be answered.

PART II
NEONATAL/INFANT STIMULATION

THE CHILD-HOLDING PATTERNS
OF THE EFE FORAGERS
OF ZAIRE *

Edward Z. Tronick, Ph.D.,
S. W. Winn, M.S.,
and Gilda Morelli, Ph.D.

How much are infants in contact with others during their first years? How much and what kinds of touch do they receive? Is much of this touch affectionate? How much of it is simply contact with another person and how much is a more vigorous form of physical stimulation? How do the form, pattern, and quality of touch differ in different cultures and with age?

This paper reports the time infants spend in various forms of contact with others within a previously described system of multiple caretaking (Tronick, Morelli, & Winn, 1987), among a foraging people of Zaire. From young infancy to the third year, there are changes not only in the percentage of time the child is held but in who is doing the holding and the affective tone of the holding.

*ACKNOWLEDGMENTS This research was supported by grants from the NICHD and NSF.

The Efe

The Efe are one of four groups of Mbuti (Pygmies) who inhabit the Ituri Forest of northeastern Zaire. Their history is the subject of much speculation; it is not known whether they once lived deep within the forest or on the border between forest and savanna, or whether they subsisted solely by hunting and gathering or were in association with agricultural peoples. However their ancestors lived, in all probability their life-style was to some unknown extent both similar and dissimilar to that of the Efe today.

Although the Efe hunt and gather forest foods, they rely on cultivated foods for their caloric intake (Bailey & Peacock, in press). They acquire these foods primarily from a Sudanic-speaking agricultural group, the Balese, who trade their produce for Efe forest foods and products and for labor. In general, a longstanding reciprocal relationship exists between members of an Efe band and a single Balese village, except during periods of food scarcity, when an Efe band may draw on the resources of several villages. Efe camps, which move every four to six weeks, are generally located within a day's walk of the village.

Camp membership ranges from 6 to 50 people and is often made up of one or several extended families, each consisting of brothers and their wives, children, unmarried sisters, and parents. Women from one band are exchanged by their male relatives for wives from another band. Members of the extended family build their huts close together, but the basic social unit of the Efe band is not the extended family but the nuclear family.

Efe life is one of continuous social interaction and exposure. Huts tend to be small — 1.5 meters in diameter and 1.15 meters in height — and to have dim interiors with few material goods. Hut use is limited to sleeping, food storage, and protection from the rain. Other activities such as eating, cooking, bathing, and child care take place in the open, and most out-of-camp activities are also shared. It is very unusual to find an Efe in a solitary setting or engaged in a solitary task.

Methods in the Study

Naturalistic observations of infants were the primary form of data collection. There were two different age cohorts. The first cohort was a longitudinal study of 10 Efe infants, 6 females and 4 males. The infants, selected from 7 different camps, were observed for 2 hours at 3 weeks of age (N = 7, mean age = 23 days, range 13-31); 2 hours at 7 weeks (N = 8, mean age = 51 days, range 43-57); and 4 hours at 18 weeks (N = 9, mean age = 137 days, range 120-152). All observations took place in the camps. The second cohort was seen cross-sectionally. It consisted of 8 children seen at 1 year, 7 at 2 years, and 8 at 3 years of age. These children were observed throughout the day for 48 hours for the 1-year-olds, 41 hours for the 2-year-olds, and 48 hours for the 3-year-olds, in a variety of settings.

Observers noted the incidence during 1-minute intervals of specific behaviors that were initiated by, or directed to, the infant. A total of 203 hours of observations was collected. Interobserver reliability sessions were conducted in the field, and reliability coefficients were found to be satisfactory on all codes.

Behavioral Codes

The behavioral coding system coded who the infant was with, what they were doing together, the affect expressed, and who initiated the activity. It coded the activities of more than one interactant at the same time. The coding schemes for the younger and older infants differed slightly because of behavioral differences related to development, but in this report they have been combined. The following codes are reported below:

> *Caretaking/holding:* Tending to a child's needs, including dressing, feeding, bathing, medical attention, and attempting to comfort a fussy or distressed infant. For the younger infant, these activities are always performed while the child is being held, whereas the child one year and older may or may not actually be held during the activity.

> *Grooming:* Picking at and removing dirt and insects from the infant. Grooming has an affectionate quality, and it is not always apparent that it is really being done for functional reasons.

Physical contact: Simple touching and leaning against, as well as more active stimulation such as bouncing and shaking.

Affectionate contact: Gentle touches with hand or mouth.

These codes capture most but not all the physical contact a child experiences, especially for the younger child. They omit, for younger infants, adjusting position, and for older children, assisting the child in negotiating an obstacle, play codes that may involve a great deal of contact, and agonistic encounters such as fighting. More than one of these codes may occur simultaneously.

Results and Discussion

Figure 3 shows the proportion of intervals Efe infants are in social contact over the first three years of life. This measure of social contact is a composite of the other measures. Note that because this behavior was coded on an interval basis, receiving and not receiving caretaking/holding can occur within a single interval; that is, in a given minute an infant might be in social contact and also left alone, and both events could be noted for that interval, so that the total can be more than 100 percent. The very young infant is in contact with someone in almost 100 percent of all intervals but was also observed to be alone in about 3 percent of the intervals. Over the course of the first year, there is a significant drop in how much the infant is in social contact, and the

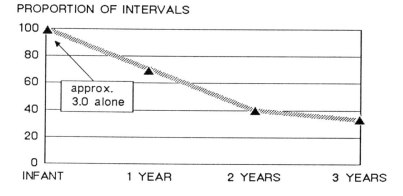

Figure 3. Proportion of intervals Efe infants are in social contact with any caretaker.

drop continues from year 1 to year 3. In the third year, the child is in social contact about 33 percent of the time. Figure 4 shows that in infancy the child's social contact is provided somewhat equally by mother and others but as the infant gets older, others provide more

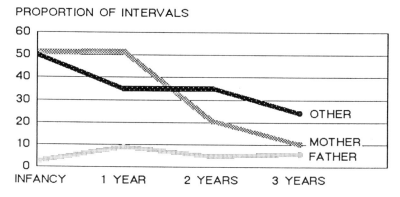

PROPORTION OF INTERVALS

Figure 4. Proportion of intervals Efe infants are in social contact with mother, father, and others.

of the social contact. Fathers provide very little contact at any age.

Figure 5 presents findings on physical contact other than as a component of social contact. In the infancy period, such contact occurs while the infant is already being held, and instances of contact that would be seen easily at older ages may go unobserved. The proportion is quite low during infancy, although the infant is being

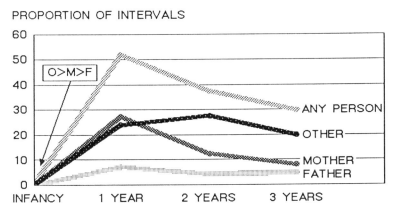

PROPORTION OF INTERVALS

Figure 5. Proportion of intervals Efe infants are in incidental physical contact.

held almost all the time, but it approaches 50 percent at 1 year and then falls off to about 30 percent at 3 years. Figure 5 also shows who engaged in this physical contact. At all ages except for infancy, others provided more physical contact than mothers or fathers.

Figure 6 presents the findings on the incidence of affectionate touch

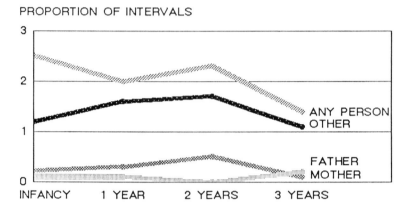

Figure 6. Proportion of intervals Efe infants receive affectionate touch.

and who engaged in affectionate touch. What is most striking is the predominance of affectionate touch engaged in by others and the decrease in affectionate touch engaged in by mothers and fathers.

Figure 7 presents the findings on grooming. Grooming drops from about 6 percent in infancy to about 2 percent in years 1 through 3. Mothers initially perform the greatest proportion of grooming, but over the first 3 years their proportion decreases and the proportion of

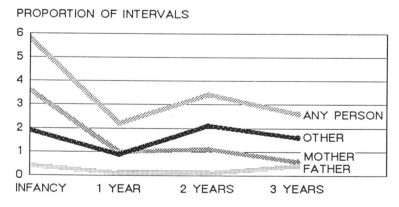

Figure 7. Proportion of intervals Efe infants are groomed.

grooming engaged in by others increases. Fathers again engage in a comparatively small proportion of grooming.

These findings present us with some striking data on the amount of contact some infants and young children receive. Over time, especially between year 1 and year 3, there is a notable decrease in the amount of contact these infants receive. Although comparative data are not available, the rates of affectionate touch and grooming seem high. Most striking is the extent to which different types of contact are engaged in by individuals other than the mother and father. In this society of foragers, infants appear to receive relatively high rates of touch from many different individuals. The fact that the Efe are a technologically simple society, supposedly living in a manner more like that of our hominid ancestors, does not make their pattern of physical contact more "natural" than others, but it raises questions about the biological functions of contact and the cultural forces that lead to different configurations in different societies.

DISCUSSION

Dr. Reite commented on the similarity in percentage of contact between the findings of this study and those in his own studies of monkeys. In monkeys, 5 months of age is about equivalent to 2 1/2 years in humans, and at that age monkeys are in contact about 50 percent of the time.

Questioned about the custom of "sister exchange," Dr. Tronick described it in somewhat more detail. Girls stay in their own bands until they are 16 or 18 years old, when they are married into other bands. In this and other Pygmy groups, the men trade their own sisters or daughters or nieces in a complicated set of obligatory economic relations. Studies now in progress are attempting to identify kinship relations among various groups and to track individual women. One interesting area for exploration is the potential situation in which a female as a 10-year-old, for example, helped care for a newborn female. If in later years the younger girl is traded into the same group that the older one married into, is there a special relationship between them?

Dr. Gewirtz wondered whether in view of the patrilineal social organization there were differences in the treatment of male and female infants. Dr. Tronick replied that with the small numbers studied so far no reliable conclusions can be drawn, but his hunch is that there are no differences.

CHILD-REARING PRACTICES AND INFANT DEVELOPMENT IN SOUTH INDIA*

Cassie Landers, Ed.D., M.P.H.

Examining culture as one of the many variables in developmental research has broadened our perspective and has increased our appreciation of the underlying processes of development. It has forced us to expand our definition of normality as we witness modes of organization that vary from one culture to another. Lester and Brazelton (1982) have designed a psychobiological model for the systematic study of infant development across cultures, to describe and document the interactions between environmental conditions of the culture, the effects of these conditions on mother and fetus, and the nature of the individual infant.

This model was applied to a group of infants born in a fishing village in South India. The study, based on the Brazelton (1973) Neonatal Behavioral Assessment Scale (NBAS) and other measures of infant

*ACKNOWLEDGMENTS The author is indebted to Dr. R.S. Iyer, of the Kasturba Medical College, Department of Pediatrics, Manipal, South India. This research was supported by the Professional Studies Program, University of California, Berkeley, and the Ford Foundation.

development, investigated the relationship between selected medical, social, and cultural variables and developmental outcome. In spite of high levels of maternal and infant risk factors, the infants studied exhibited a dramatic pattern of recovery in increased velocity of physical growth, advanced motor development, and optimal cognitive performance. This paper discusses the ability of the child-rearing patterns and practices to influence the child's development and specifically explores the impact on development of the increased levels of tactile and kinesthetic stimulation that characterize the environment of these infants.

Early Childhood in an Indian Village

The major site of the study was Malpe, a coastal village in Karnataka State in South India with about 17,000 inhabitants, most of whom are poor fishermen of low caste. Most housing consists of small one-room huts with thatched roofs, mud or bamboo walls, and dirt floors. Few of the homes have electricity.

With rare exceptions, members of this community grow up in some form of extended family organization, either a joint family with two or more married brothers living together with their wives and children or a generational family of parents and one of their married children and his spouse and children (Kakar, 1978). The extended family is a cooperative unit whose members engage in the many activities necessary for its survival and protect its members from the uncertainty and threats of the outside world. In determining the division of labor and articulating the relationships between its members, the family relies upon a well-defined principle of hierarchy, which is inherent in all Indian society.

The infant growing up in this environment has a prolonged and deep attachment to the mother, although the extended family provides other potential caregivers. In the early years, the infant is carried astride the mother's hip and is actively engaged as she performs most of her daily chores. Continuously held, cuddled, and talked to, the infant enjoys a maternal relationship of a duration and intensity not usually found in the Western world (Kakar, 1979). Breast-feeding is on demand at all times of the day and night and often continues until the second or third year of life. Developmental accomplishments are responded to with delight, but minimal demands are placed on the child to explore and master the world independent of the mother. The parental agenda of early child development in India thus contrasts sharply with that in the West, which places a high value on predetermined goals. The Indian mother emphasizes the positive aspects of her child's behavior and accedes to the child's demands rather than attempting to control and structure them.

Sample Characteristics and Methodology of the Study

The subjects were 30 full-term infants who had had normal deliveries and whose mothers had uncomplicated medical histories. Birthweights ranged from 2,000 grams to 3,550 grams, with a mean of 2,777 grams. Because the average birthweight of full-term infants in India is about 500 grams less than that in Western countries, infants less than 2,500 grams were included in the study and were not considered low birthweight (LBW). When compared with the U.S. birthweight standards, 60 percent of the male infants were at or below the 10th percentile and 40 percent were at or below the 50th percentile; 41 percent of the female infants were at or below the 10th percentile and 59 percent were at or below the 50th percentile.

The ponderal index, the ratio of birthweight to body length, was used to identify fetal malnutrition. Unlike birthweight, the ponderal index is not confounded by such factors as race or sex in defining malnutrition. Babies who are long, with a relatively small amount of soft tissue mass, can be seen as having experienced a late-gestation nutritional insult (Brazelton, Parker, & Zuckerman, 1976). On the basis of research in the Western world, a ponderal index less than 2.3 has been used to define fetal malnutrition in term infants. The mean ponderal index in the Indian infants in the study was 2.36, with a range of 1.88 to 3.28. When 2.3 is used as the cutoff point, 45 percent of these infants are defined as malnourished or small for gestational age (SGA).

Areas studied included behavioral organization, medical factors (both infant and maternal), psychometric factors, and sociocultural factors such as socioeconomic status, family structure, and social support system. The Brazelton NBAS was administered on days 1, 3, 5, 7, 10, and 30 of life. In analysis of the data, individual items were grouped according to the behavioral and reflex clusters developed by Lester, Als, and Brazelton (1982): *habituation*, response decrement to repeated auditory, visual, and tactile stimulation; *orientation*, response to animate and inanimate stimuli and overall alertness; *motor*, integrated motor acts and overall muscle tonus; *range of state*, the rapidity, peak, and lability of state changes; *regulation of state*, the infant's own efforts to modulate state control; *autonomic regulation*, signs of physiological stress such as tremors, startles, and changes in skin color; and *reflex*, the total number of deviant reflex scores. The Bayley Scales of Infant Development (Bayley, 1969) were administered to each infant at three months.

Brazelton NBAS Cluster Scores: Results and Interpretation

The Indian infants performed in the optimal range on the habituation cluster, which assesses the capacity to shut out disturbing visual, auditory, and tactile stimulation that might otherwise make excessive demands on the infant's immature physiologic system — a capacity that serves the infant well in the environment of small, crowded, and open huts, where the child is exposed to a continuous stream of intense stimulation. It is proposed that the practice of swaddling, used by this community, is related to this optimal habituation response. Swaddling is generally believed to have a calming, restraining influence on infants, inducing and extending sleep, reducing levels of motor activity in response to stimulation, reducing startles, and lowering heart-rate variability (Chisholm, 1978; Lipton, Steinschneider, & Richmond, 1965).

By contrast, orientation scores fell at the low- to mid-range level of the scale, although there was large within-group variation. Two possible explanations are offered. One hypothesis involves the less-than-ideal conditions under which the examination was performed. Although ideally the infant should be assessed between feedings and in a quiet and dimly lit environment, demand feeding and the stimulation provided by the surrounding activities and multiple observers made it more difficult for the examiner to bring the infant to the quiet alert state needed to elicit the infant's optimal response. The second hypothesis relates to maternal expectations for the social responsivity of the infant. In the first month of life, there was little face-to-face interaction between the mother and her infant. Caregiving activities concentrated on ministering to the infant's physiologic needs; maternal vocalizations were rare, and while the mother observed the infant, it was without any expectation of response.

The performance of these infants in the motor cluster was particularly noteworthy. The motor activity exhibited by this group could be qualitatively described as mature, somewhat hypertonic, and resistant, with an air of deliberate intensity. Movements were not the jerky motions with restricted arcs characteristic of the immature infant, nor were they the smooth, well-controlled movements typifying the healthy full-term infant. Rather, their vigorous, intensely driving responses were indicative of strong motoric potential. Largely controlled by state behavior, most motor activity was seen when the infant was roused to active fussy or crying states. Nonpurposeful activity was rarely seen during sleep and quiet alert states. The infants were easily consoled through appropriately supportive tactile maneuvers. Comparative data from a group of Caucasian American middle-class infants show that while the U.S. infants perform significantly better on the pull-to-sit item on day 1, by day 10 the Indian infants' performance was significantly better (figure 8; Landers, 1983).

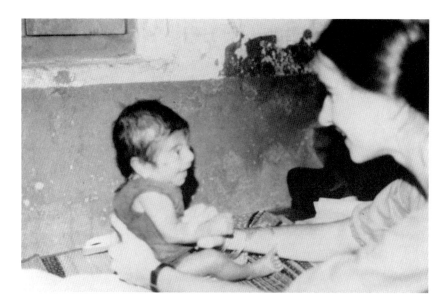

Figure 8.   One-month-old infant showing marked head control during pull-to-sit.

It was suggested that the superior performance of the Indian infants by day 10 is evidence for the interplay of their given biologic potential for early motor development and the type and quality of environmental stimulation they received. The Indian infants' needs were typically tended to with quick, abrupt, and vigorous movements. This type of motor stimulation was most noticeable during the bathing of the infants. The Indian bath, which has been described by other investigators (Hopkins, 1976; Leboyer, 1976), is an elaborate, formal routine of daily massage that begins in the first few days of life and continues throughout the first year. The infant is placed prone on the mother's outstretched legs, and each part of the body is in turn individually stretched and prodded. With tepid water and soap, the lower extremities are massaged first, followed by the arms, back, abdomen, neck, and face. Exhausted from the intensity of this stimulation, the infant is swaddled and enters into a prolonged sleep.

Figure 9. Daily infant bath and massage performed by maternal grandmother.

The abrupt handling of the infant was observed only during caregiving activities; no other efforts at stimulation were made. Moreover, the infant's motor activity was usually interpreted as a signal of distress, to which the mother responded with feeding and/or rocking. To console by rocking, the mother placed the infant upright on her outstretched legs and instigated rocking movements by tapping the infant's back, requiring the infant to maintain adequate head and neck control.

In the range of state cluster, the Indian infants were somewhat irritable and hypersensitive to stimulation as they moved rapidly into an intense cry state, where they were unavailable to respond and interact with the external environment. Their mean scores in this cluster showed no significant improvement over time, although strong within-group differences may have been operative.

Regulation of state showed a decreasing trend between day 1 and day 30. Infants performed in the middle to upper range of the scale throughout the first 10 days of life and in response to being cuddled they reacted almost instantly by nestling in the crook of the examiner's neck. Even during the first or second examination an infant would spontaneously bring his or her state under control with hand-to-mouth movements.

Autonomic regulation, as measured by tremulousness, amount of startle during an examination, and lability of skin color, was in the optimal range on day 1 and increased up through day 7, when it stabilized. Again, these responses may be related to the practice of swaddling and support the findings of other investigators (Brackbill, 1973; Giacoman, 1971; Lipton, Steinschneider, & Richmond, 1965).

Finally, the reflex cluster showed a significant pattern of recovery in reflex activity during the first month of life. Of the 16 elicited reflexes, an increased sucking/rooting response, decreased walking/stepping, and incurvation response accounted for most of the deviation in the early days of life. The exaggerated sucking and rooting responses can be related to hunger and rate of milk flow (Brazelton, Parker, & Zuckerman, 1976), and in the early examinations these infants did show signs of hunger. The hypotonic walking and stepping responses seen early on may also be the result of depleted nutritional stores as a result of poor intrauterine growth. Incurvation of the trunk often did not appear until day 5 or day 7, but this response is often weak or absent in the first few days (Prechtl & Beintema, 1964), and the decreased response was not considered abnormal.

Development at Three Months

The velocity of growth in the infants during the first 3 months of life was quite remarkable. Weight at 3 months ranged from 4.0 kg to 8.0 kg, with a mean of 5.92 kg. When the weights of the Indian infants were compared with U.S. standards, the following picture emerged. Of the 17 boys, 4 were above the 90th percentile, 5 fell between the 50th and 90th percentiles, 4 were between the 10th and 50th percentiles, and 4 fell below the 10th percentile. Of the girls, 4 were above the 90th percentile, 4 were between the 50th and 90th percentiles, and 4 were between the 10th and 50th percentiles. Only 1 child fell below the 10th percentile. The average weight gain was 3.16 kg, whereas average weight gain for U.S. infants is 2.5 kg (Lowrey, 1973). According to Western pediatric standards, birthweight should double by 5 months (Lowrey, 1973). In this sample, 65 percent had doubled their birthweights by 3 months. Two additional measures of infant growth—length and head circumference—showed similar increases in the first 3 months.

The Bayley Scales (1969) were administered to each infant at age 3 months, and the Mental Development Index (MDI) and Psychomotor Development Index (PDI) were calculated. These indices are a normalized standard score with a mean of 100 and a range of 50 to 150. For this sample, the mean MDI was 108.6, with a range of 72-131. The motor index yielded a slightly higher mean score of 129.2 and a range that spanned the entire scale. Twenty-three percent of the Indian infants had a motor index of 140 or above, a score achieved by fewer than 10 percent of U.S. infants. While the Indian infants performed similarly to U.S. infants in tasks of cognitive development, specific items of the motor scale were in advance of the norms. These included the gross motor abilities such as head balance, sitting alone momentarily, and rolling over from back to stomach. More than 50 percent of the Indian infants passed these items at age 3 months, whereas the mean ages for the standardized U.S. sample are 4.2, 5.3, and 6.4 months, respectively. In fine motor performance, partial thumb opposition while holding a cube was more advanced for the Indian sample.

In summary, the data described a growth pattern of a group of infants that was characterized by a dramatic rate of physical growth, advanced motor performance, and patterns of cognitive development similar to the standards defined by U.S. infants. This pattern of development in the first three months mirrors the course of adaptation witnessed in the first month of life.

Conclusions

The findings of this study, although exploratory in nature, challenge a number of widely accepted assumptions concerning the relationship between pre- and perinatal circumstances and infant growth. In accepting this challenge, one is required to acknowledge a number of models that may be operative. The data lend themselves to the consideration of three perspectives: (1) the efficacy and adaptability of the biological organism to overcome the demands of a stressful environment; (2) the effectiveness of culturally adapted infant-rearing patterns; and (3) the unique psychological makeup and identity development of the Indian woman.

Biological adaptability. The behavior of this group of infants exemplifies the adaptability of the human infant confronted with persistent stress to return to a predetermined developmental pathway. This process was particularly salient in the dramatic catch-up weight gain during the first three months of life. It is argued that the biological capacity for catch-up growth is inherent in our species, and the maternal feeding practices allowed this preprogrammed adaptability to unfold. Unlike most rural mothers in India, who do not give colostrum (Agarwal & Agarwal, 1981), these mothers began breast-feeding within 24 to 48 hours, providing antibodies and other components which serve to defend against infection (Goldman & Smith, 1973; Gyorgy, 1967; Jelliffe & Jelliffe, 1971; Lozoff et al., 1977; Stohiar et al., 1976). A significantly enhanced resistance to enteric infection has been observed among breast-fed babies, not only when the environment is favorable but also when environmental sanitation is at less than acceptable levels (Mata, 1978; Mata & Wyatt, 1971). In addition, these mothers nursed their infants frequently, on demand. The low-fat, low-protein composition of human breast milk suggests that this is the pattern for which evolution has adapted us (see Kennell, this volume). When viewed in this light, the ability of these small infants to exhibit catch-up growth is simply part of the developmental script of the human species. Early deviations from expected patterns of growth can be seen as a result of environmental forces that constrain and defeat the organism's self-righting tendencies and inherent ability to return to the path of normality (Sameroff, 1975).

Child-rearing patterns. In this highly supportive environment, even the most vulnerable infants were integrated into the family in a manner that fostered their capacity for recovery. LeVine (1977) has commented that "cultural evolution within human populations also produces standardized strategies of survival for infants and children, strategies reflecting environmental pressures from a more recent past, encoded in customs rather than genes and transmitted socially rather than biologically" (p. 16).

The motoric stimulation received by these infants, reflected in the elaborate daily bath and massage, seemed particularly well suited to these motorically precocious infants and paved the way for increasingly complex motor organization. Active stimulation was complemented by swaddling techniques that seemed to be related to an increased capacity to habituate to disturbing stimulation and maintain autonomic regulation. Other cross-cultural studies (Super, 1981a, 1981b) have reported rapid motor development in infancy in cultures where an increased amount of kinesthetic stimulation, maternal proximity, and rapid response to distress signals are the norm. These findings have been confirmed by numerous experimental studies of human infants given supplemental kinesthetic stimulation (Ambrose, 1969; Brossard & De Carie, 1968; Korner & Thoman, 1972; Scarr-Salapatek & Williams, 1973; Yarrow, Rubenstein, & Pedersen, 1975).

The type and quality of maternal social responsivity also constitute an adaptive pattern. The mother's immediate response to distress signals is an adaptive reaction to the pressures of a harsh physical environment and at the same time conforms to the culture's value for dependency rather than autonomous functioning. Several investigators (Lewin & Goldberg, 1969; Yarrow, Rubenstein, & Pedersen, 1975) have found a positive correlation between maternal contingent responsiveness and infant cognitive development.

Maternal commitment. The Indian mother has a powerful psychosocial commitment to the survival of her infant. The pattern of responsivity toward the infant reflects not only her deeply rooted emotional stance toward her child but the culture's perception of and value for the child, which is closely tied up with her own identity development.

It is only with motherhood that the Indian woman comes into her own and establishes her position within the family and community (Kakar, 1978).

Thus, as these data emphasize, the application of universal risk factors in development must be viewed with caution, for the mechanisms through which they exert their effect vary both between and within cultures. For a given factor, the degree of risk imposed is directly related to the culturally defined structures and institutions that have evolved to buffer its impact. We must continue to construct paradigms that allow for the systematic analysis of the contexts that directly and indirectly influence the developmental pathway.

DISCUSSION

Much of the discussion focused on the concept of catch-up growth in the cultural context. Is it appropriate, several participants asked, to refer to growth in relation to Western norms as "catch-up"? The term "catch-up" also implies that there was severe malnutrition from which the infants recovered. The infants' ponderal index, as measured by Western standards, indicated that they were malnourished in utero, but again participants questioned the validity of using Western norms to define risk factors in the Third World. How would these infants have compared with norms based on a middle- or upper-middle-class population from Bombay or Delhi?

Dr. Brazelton agreed that it would be useful to have a comparison with an optimal group of newborns. Studies are available that conclude that birthweight of Indian infants increases with increased socioeconomic status. He estimated that at least 50 to 60 percent of the Indian population with low socioeconomic status experiences the intrauterine undernutrition that was postulated in this group. Whether or not the term "catch-up" is appropriate, Dr. Landers stressed, the important point to be seen in the study is the tremendous spurt in weight gain achieved by these babies in the first three months and the cultural adaptations that have evolved to foster this development.

Dr. Oller suggested that what was represented in the infants in the sample might be simply a different pattern of growth. Dr. Brazelton noted, however, that there was other evidence of nutritional deprivation among these babies: the skin on their hands and feet and around the umbilicus was peeling, as is characteristic of late intrauterine deprivation; they had worried looks, and they had other signs characteristic of babies in our culture who are below the 10th percentile.

DOULA-MOTHER AND PARENT-INFANT CONTACT*

John H. Kennell, M.D.

When birth moved from the home to the hospital in the twentieth century, spectacular improvements in maternal and infant mortality resulted. In the process, however, numerous traditions and practices affecting the mother, the infant, and the mother-infant pair were lost. Clinical research and studies of nonindustrial societies in which these traditions are still practiced suggest that this loss is a significant one, and human touch appears again and again as a critical component of the lost interactions. This paper reviews a number of perinatal research studies in which tactile contact is shown as a key element in the significant interactions that occur at the beginning of human life.

Anthropologic data suggest that the human species has not significantly changed physiologically or genetically for one to two million years. Throughout this period, humans have had the same skull and bone structure, the same number of chromosomes, and perhaps many of the same behavior patterns. During most of this time they lived as hunters and gatherers (see figure 10), and human physiologic proc-

*ACKNOWLEDGMENTS Many of the studies reported were conducted with Marshall H. Klaus and more recently also with Susan McGrath. The research was made possible by a currently active grant, NICHD R01 16915-05, and grants from the Arthur Vining Davis Foundations; the Thrasher Research Fund; Pittway Corporation Charitable Foundation; Department of Health and Human Services, Division of Maternal & Child Health, Public Health Services Grants; the William T. Grant Foundation; the Research Foundation; and the Robert Wood Johnson Foundation.

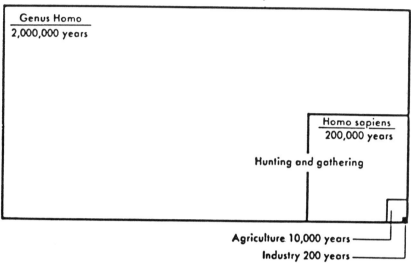

Figure 10. Schematic diagram illustrating the relative time humans have spent as industrial and agricultural societies and as hunters and gatherers. (From "Birth and 'Bonding' in Non-Industrial Societies" by M. Lozoff, *Developmental Medicine and Child Neurology* 25, p. 595. Copyright 1983, MacKeith Press, London)

esses and genetic makeup evolved in adaptation to that life style (Lozoff, 1983). This long history of evolutionary adaptation, during which biology, molded by the environment, slowly evolved practices related to childbirth and child-rearing, has provided the conceptual framework for productive research. Observations of the behavior of hunters and gatherers and of agricultural societies have generated questions about human physiological processes that could then be tested in industrial societies.

The Doula: Support During Labor

In 127 out of 128 representative nonindustrial societies, a woman is present with the mother-to-be during labor; in only one society does the mother labor alone. Prior to the twentieth century, it was also the practice in our society for family members to support the mother actively in labor. Although more fathers and others have been allowed into labor and delivery rooms in the last 20 years, a considerable number of mothers still go through childbirth without the presence of family members or close friends.

In a study of 417 healthy women in an obstetric setting in Guatemala, we systematically examined the clinical effects of continuous social support during labor and delivery (Klaus et al., 1986). The experimental group received support from a woman who was not a midwife, physician, or nurse. This supportive companion, whom we have called a *doula*, stayed close to the laboring woman, stroking, holding, and talking to her. The control group of mothers labored alone, according to routine practice.

Several highly significant differences were seen. The 168 women receiving support had fewer perinatal complications (34 percent versus 74 percent for the control group). Medication was prescribed more often in the control group (19 percent versus 4 percent in the treatment group). The rate of cesarean section was greater in the control group (19 percent versus 7 percent in the treatment group). With a continuous caregiver length of labor was shorter (averaging 8 hours versus 14 hours for those without such support). Moreover, there was also a trend for a smaller percentage of the infants from the experimental group to be admitted to the neonatal intensive care unit (2.4 versus 6.8 percent).

A more recent study (Kennell et al., 1988) conducted in the United States again showed that support by a doula during labor and delivery had highly significant benefits to the mother and infant. In spite of the measures used in modern obstetric care to shorten the length of labor — such as artificial rupture of membranes, use of oxytocin and forceps, and cesarean delivery — none of these interventions resulted in as short a labor length as did the presence of a doula. Unexpectedly fewer babies of mothers who had support required an extended hospital stay.

What does a doula do that is associated with such powerful effects? As part of our U.S. study, Terri DeLay conducted a time sampling study (DeLay, Kennell, & Klaus, 1987) of the activities of three experienced doulas during early labor (4 to 6 cm. cervical dilatation) and later labor (7 to 10 cm. cervical dilatation). Doulas spent the majority of the time within one foot of the laboring woman; as labor progressed, they increased the time spent within one inch of her. Almost half the time they talked with the mother, comforting, encour-

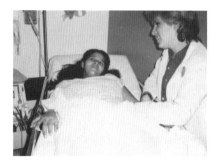
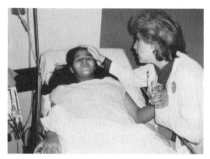

Figure 11. Doulas talking with, stroking, and holding mothers
during labor. As labor
progresses, a doula spends
an increasing amount of
time within one inch of
the mother.

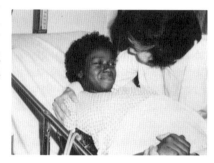

aging, and instructing her, to reduce her anxiety either directly or indirectly by distracting her from the pain. Over half the time the doulas
used various styles of touching the mother: rubbing and stroking her
head, clutching or holding her extremities, and both rubbing/stroking
and clutching/holding her trunk (figure 11). They touched the mother
significantly more during contractions; in early labor they used more
rubbing and stroking, while in late labor they clutched and held her
more.

In addition to the direct effects reported above, we have found that
the continuous support of a doula appears to have indirect effects that
influence early mother-infant communication and facilitate a mother's
early attachment to her baby (Sosa et al., 1980). The mothers who had
a doula present during labor were awake more of the time they were
with their newborns in the first 22.5 minutes after they left the delivery
room, if we carefully controlled for length of labor. They stroked,
smiled at, and talked to their babies significantly more than the control
mothers when we controlled for length of labor and the time the

mothers were awake. We have no evidence to indicate whether this interaction has long-term implications, but clues in an early study (Klaus et al., 1972) suggest that the level of tactile involvement between mothers and infants during the early postpartum period might significantly affect later behavior. In a recent study (Kaitz et al., 1989), postpartum women who had been exposed to their infants for at least one hour were able to identify their own babies out of three newborns by touching their hands, whereas neither nonparturient women nor men could do so at a rate that exceeded chance.

Species-specific Behavior

Specific kinds of maternal behavior such as nesting, retrieving, grooming, and exploring are seen in nonhuman mammals immediately before, during, and after delivery. These have evolved to meet the needs of the young in the animal's usual environment. We wondered whether human mothers displayed similar species-specific behavior. A stimulus to explore this subject was provided by the unusual behavior we observed in the mothers of premature infants during the first days and weeks of life. On the first visit, mothers walked around the incubator rather warily. When shown how to put their hands into the incubator, they would only briefly and hesitantly poke the baby's extremities with their fingertips (Barnett et al., 1970). We decided to examine in detail the behavior of mothers of full-term and premature infants during the first minutes and hours of their initial interactions.

When the mothers of the full-term infants first saw their infants, an orderly and predictable pattern of behavior was observed. Commencing hesitantly with fingertip contact on the extremities, within four or five minutes they began caressing the trunk with the palm, simultaneously showing progressively heightened excitement, which continued for several minutes. By the end of nine minutes, fingertip touch had dropped substantially and palm contact more than doubled, and a similar shift was seen from touching the infant's extremities to touching the infant's trunk (Klaus et al., 1970).

Mothers of premature infants, studied on their first three contacts (over a period of from 1 to 17 days), exhibited an attenuated sequence of this behavior. Touch was much more limited, even in the third visit, and neither the progression from fingertip to palm contact nor the shift from extremity touch to trunk touch occurred over the first three visits. Instead, all types of touch increased gradually (Klaus & Kennell, 1982).

At present it is not possible to state whether there are specific patterns of behavior after delivery in the human or how one would go about determining whether or not the observed behavior is characteristic. It is, however, interesting to see recurring patterns in different delivery situations, both hospital and home, in the United States.

Bonding

Of the standard anthropologic sample of 186 representative non-industrial societies, 183 societies expect mothers and babies to nest together for days or weeks after delivery; virtually none permits the degree of separation that has been routine in many maternity hospitals in this century. In recent years, numerous studies (reviewed in Klaus & Kennell, 1982) have examined whether additional time for close contact between mother and infant in the first minutes, hours, and days of life alters the quality of attachment.

In one study, extra time for mother-infant contact was added not only during the first three hours after delivery but also during the next three days. Both one month later and one year later, the mothers in the group who had had extra contact showed significantly more affectionate behavior toward their infants than those in the control group.

In 13 studies, the additional contact occurred only during the first hour of life. In 10 of these studies significant differences in maternal behavior were noted. In 6 of the 9 studies that examined breast-feeding patterns, the duration of breast-feeding was significantly increased in the experimental group.

The effects of increased mother-infant contact in these 17 studies may be due in part to a recapitulation of what was previously normal human maternal behavior. Increasing mother-infant contact anytime during the first three postpartum days may trip an innate system in women that has been present in our genetic makeup for centuries and may in part compensate for the marked deprivation that is characteristic of present-day hospital routine.

Support and Mother-Infant Interaction

Anisfeld and Lipper (1983) showed that a group of mothers who had contact with their infants in the first hour after delivery showed much more affectionate interaction with their infant 48 hours after delivery than mothers who experienced routine separation. Analysis of their data revealed that these effects were strikingly increased with those mothers who had a low level of social support, as defined by two or more of the following: they were single; they were on public assistance; they had not graduated from high school; and they did not have the father or other family member present in the delivery room. In contrast, mothers with this same lack of social support who experienced routine separation after delivery showed the lowest level of affectionate interaction with their newborns.

Carrying, Communication, and Breast-Feeding

The practice of our hunter-gatherer ancestors of carrying the baby on the mother's body and sleeping with the baby at night is still carried out in developing countries with a settled agricultural existence. Travelers to these countries are amazed to note that they never hear a baby cry. In our society, mothers use the baby's scream as a cue to communication, but in many cultures the mother learns to pick up tactile signals as she carries the infant on her body all day. She is expected to detect the small changes in breathing and body movements that precede urination and defecation, so that by the end of one week she is able to care for her baby with no soiling of her clothes; she is considered a poor mother if she makes a misjudgment.

Barr has carefully studied the behavior of infants and mothers of the !Kung hunters and gatherers. He reports that in the first three months infants cry or fuss 17 times an hour on average and the caregiver responds 92 percent of the time (Barr, Bakeman, Konner, & Adamson, 1987).

When the mother is breast-feeding and the infant is carried on her body, there is no delay when the baby becomes hungry. Thoman (1975b) in home observations found that an infant would stop crying promptly if the mother intervened within the first 90 seconds; crying was greatly prolonged if she did not tend to the baby's crying within that time.

Carrying and feeding practices that have been maintained over hundreds of thousands of years may prove to have physiological and adaptive advantages. Observations of women and their babies in hunting-gathering and agricultural societies reveal that they may nurse 30 to 40 times in 24 hours, each time for a short period. Studies exploring the effect of increasing the feeding frequency of nursing mothers have provided a new understanding of several neonatal physiologic processes. In one study (de Carvalho et al., 1983), mothers who were encouraged to nurse frequently in the first two weeks (9.9 feedings per 24 hours) produced significantly more milk than mothers breast-feeding on a three- to four-hour schedule (7.3 feedings per 24 hours), and their babies gained more weight. In a second study, infants of mothers who nursed their babies more than 8 times per 24 hours in the first three days of life had significantly lower serum bilirubin levels (de Carvalho, Klaus, & Merkatz, 1982).

Evidence from comparative physiology gives further support for increasing feeding frequencies. Measurements of the fat and protein constituents of milk from many mammals suggest that the human pattern of infant care in the past was nearly continuous feeding and carrying. Infant animals in species such as deer that are adapted for long separations (feeding every 4 to 12 hours) receive milk with a high protein and fat concentration and reduced water, whereas infant mammals who are carried or follow their mothers and feed almost continuously receive milk with a low protein and fat concentration. Human milk is low in fat and extremely low in protein. It is therefore suggested that human babies were probably carried and nursed frequently for more than 99 percent of our species' existence (Lozoff et al., 1977).

Conclusions

Human mothers, fathers, and infants have a wide range of adaptability. Modern adaptations in the care of parents and newborn infants may have considerable cost. The studies reported here have yielded valuable biobehavioral findings, but they do not necessarily suggest what should be recommended behavior in our industrialized society. The striking similarity of some of the touching and physical contact behaviors across many cultures other than our own suggests that these behaviors may have biological survival value and may more often be linked to generalizable physiological or biological principles. Explorations of other biological systems associated with the behavior of hunters and gatherers as well as the almost universal practices in agricultural societies may provide a valuable guide to creative and novel studies of touch and human contact that could further benefit mothers, fathers, and infants throughout the world.

DISCUSSION

Much of the discussion focused on the role of the doula in relation to that of the father, who today is frequently present at the birth. Is the father adequately prepared to function as the doula? Does his presence have the same effects, such as shortening labor? Dr. Kennell reported that in interviews of parents after delivery at which the fathers had been present, both mothers and fathers felt that the father's presence had been very important, even when he had done little to support his wife. It is not yet known whether benefits similar to those produced by the doula result from the presence of the father, but studies are now being done to try to determine that.

Fathers are quite different from doulas, Dr. Kennell noted. If it is their first baby (and in the research reported here the births were all first babies), the father is just as inexperienced and frightened as the mother. The mother often worries about him, urging him to rest or get something to eat, in a total reversal of the idea of support. A doula has been through labors and deliveries before and is not tense. Moreover, she is committed to staying with the mother throughout labor and delivery; fathers often have to break away, and it is when the going gets toughest that they are most likely to leave.

Ms. Evans, reporting from the experience of both being a doula and having a doula at childbirth, stressed the importance of the woman-to-woman relationship, and Dr. Kennell agreed. It is very hard for a woman to relax totally with her sexual partner and to share all the physiological phenomena that may occur. Individual differences are important, however. Dr. Kennell noted that a pilot study to examine the behavior of male partners during labor and delivery (Nagashima et al., 1987) found some fathers providing excellent support while others fell short. Experiences with the doula supporting both mother and father during labor and delivery suggest that the doula's support may enable the father to be more supportive toward his wife.

What value does society place on the doula? It varies from place to place, Dr. Kennell commented. In some cities it is popular. There may be a doula coordinator who finds someone to serve as a doula for a mother in labor, with the expectation that that mother in turn will later provide support for someone else. In other places people pay for the doula. The use of the doula may reduce hospital expenses and obstetricians' fees, he noted. That point led into a discussion of changes in hospital practices with regard to birth. While some innovations are becoming fairly routine, such as the presence of fathers in labor and delivery and mothers' getting their babies sooner, Dr. Kennell expressed concern about what he called the "medicalization" of birth, such as the frequent use of epidural anesthesia, routine monitoring of births, and very high incidence of cesarean section. "We gain a little," he commented, "but I think we've got to worry about losing more than we've gained from some of those obstetric interventions when applied to low-risk mothers."

EFFECTS ON PARENTS OF CONTACT/TOUCH IN THE FIRST POSTPARTUM HOUR*

Jacob L. Gewirtz, Ph.D.,
and Albert R. Hollenbeck, Ph.D.

In recent years, much attention has been directed to the importance of physical contact and touch between parents and neonate in the first hours and days of life, particularly for the later bonding of mother to

*ACKNOWLEDGMENTS The authors wish to thank S. Lawson Sebris and Robert L. Manniello, who played important roles in the initiation phase of the study. Ms. Sebris also oversaw the data collection scheduling. In addition, we are grateful to those who helped in the collection of the data: Jeanne Adams, Elizabeth Boyd, Carol Wegley Brown, Christine Davenport, Eileen Fishbein, Cheryl Maltz, Anne Mayfield, Sherry Thrasher, and Joyce Winston.

infant (deChateau, 1976; Gewirtz & Boyd, 1977; Klaus et al., 1972). In this paper, we examine the effects of contact during the first postpartum hour on parent satisfaction and parent and neonate behavior during the first month.

Touch and physical contact were involved in two ways in this study: among the *treatment variables*, involving different degrees and durations of mother-neonate bodily and social contact in the recovery room, or between father and neonate in the special-care nursery, and, at 28 days postpartum, as some of the *outcome variables* of the differential treatments, which included parent fingering, palming, kissing, smiling, and giving care to the infant.

Methods of the Study

Two groups of infants and parents were studied, 62 vaginally delivered middle-class women and their neonates and 35 middle-class couples and their neonates delivered by elective cesarean section. In the vaginal deliveries (VD), the interaction during the first hour postpartum was between the mother and her infant, who was either swaddled and nested in the mother's arm or placed naked in a ventral-ventral position with head aligned on the mother's naked body, for either 15 minutes or 60 minutes in the recovery room. In the cesarean section deliveries (CSD), the father interacted with his neonate for either 5 minutes or up to 60 minutes (mean 37 minutes) via isolette sleeves during the first postpartum hour as the infant lay in the isolette in a special-care nursery. Outcomes were assessed in interchange with mothers during 15-minute feed and 15-minute nonfeed settings and, in the case of the CSD group, in the nonfeed setting with fathers, at two points, day 2 or 3 and day 28 of the neonate's life. Scores were the frequency of 10-second time units in which a behavior was observed at least once.

Multivariate analyses of covariance (MANCOVA) were conducted to determine whether the parental and neonate behaviors observed in the recovery room and special-care nursery were accounted for by such variables as gender, parity, pre- and postpartum medication, and anesthesia. In the case of VD infants, after correcting for post-delivery medications received by the mother, the MANCOVA yielded a treatment main effect only for duration of physical contact for both mother and infant. Not unexpectedly, given the greater opportunity with time, the number of time units in which there occurred the mother's contact behaviors of fingering, palming, kissing, and giving care showed reliably higher means in the group that had 60-minute contact than the group that had 15-minute contact; the same pattern of reliable results held for the more distal behaviors of smiling, grimacing, looking at, talking to, vocalizing to, and showing and telling. Similarly, infants in the 60-minute group displayed reliably higher frequency of grimaces, eyes open, nonvocal sounds, mouthings, fussing/crying, motor acts, and feeding than those in the 15-minute group. No difference was found in contact behavior patterns between the swaddled/nested and naked/aligned VD conditions.

Paternal behavior with the CSD infants followed the same pattern as maternal behavior with the VD infants. A MANCOVA followed by univariate analyses showed that higher mean time-block frequencies of fingering, palming, and rocking the newborn, as well as the more distal behaviors of looking at the neonate, were manifested by the fathers in the group that had the longer duration of contact. Among the CSD infants, after parity of the neonate was controlled for, more grimaces, *en face* looking, eyes open, nonvocal sounds, mouthings, fussing/crying, and motor acts were exhibited by the group with longer duration of contact.

Parental Satisfaction with the Infant

In a home visit 28 days after delivery, ratings were made by a female interviewer using 11 rating scales of parent behavior and orientation developed by Yarrow, Rubenstein, and Pedersen (1975) and revised by Vietze (personal communication, 1977). Only one of these scales contributed reliable MANCOVA results: Within the CSD group, a main effect was found for fathers over mothers on the scale measuring the parent's satisfaction with the baby's personality; fathers were rated as manifesting a higher mean satisfaction with their babies' habits of sleeping, feeding, excreting, socializing, smiling, fussing, playing, and general responsiveness (figure 12). (No parallel comparison between mothers and fathers in the VD group could be made in the context of this study.)

This finding presents a paradox. In the CSD group, it was the fathers

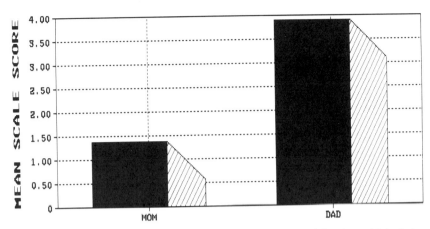

Figure 12. Parent ratings in cesarean section group: Satisfaction with baby's personality at 28 days.

and not the mothers who had the contact with their newborns in the first hour postpartum. If such contact in the earliest life phase is important, it makes sense that these fathers would show more satisfaction than the mothers with their babies' personality. On that basis, however, the VD mothers who had 15 or 60 minutes of physical/social contact with their infants in the first postpartum hour would be expected to be more satisfied with their babies' personality than the CSD mothers, who did not see their babies for hours and in some cases for two or three days after delivery. Yet no difference in rated satisfaction with infant personality was detected between the two groups of mothers. This discrepancy remains to be explained.

A possible explanation of the finding that fathers were more satisfied with their babies' personality than mothers in the CSD group is that it is an artifact of the unique study conditions of that group. Although the rater was blind to the treatment that had been received, expectancies discerned by the rater or the father concerning the purposes of the study may have had an unintended experimental effect (see Barber, 1976, for a review of such artifactual effects). Also, demand characteristics, which are situation-produced artifacts (Orne, 1962), may have increased the ratings of the female raters observing only the CSD (and not the VD) fathers with their neonates in the home, both for the parent satisfaction analysis and for the analysis of the role of initial feeding mode that follows. Deaux's (1985) review of the gender-difference literature cites studies relating results to investigator/observer gender, raising the question as a general issue of scientific procedure for studies such as this one.

The Role of Initial Feeding Mode

An unexpected effect was found to involve the initial feeding mode (bottle or breast) employed or intended by the mother at day 2 or 3. When the variances due to the main father-versus-mother effect were removed, a number of behavior scales for CSD fathers related to initial feeding mode. CSD fathers of neonates bottle-fed at 2 to 3 days were rated at 28 days as showing more intense negative emotional expression in the presence of the neonate and as being more influenced by the observer — both negatively valued behavior patterns. In contrast, the fathers of neonates who were breast-fed at 2 to 3 days, or whose mothers at that point intended to breast-feed them, were rated at 28 days as showing the positively valued behavior patterns of more physical involvement and closeness with the neonate, more speed in responding to infant behaviors connoting distress, more frequent contingent responding to infant nondistress behavior, more appropriate behavior in initiating and managing the neonate's feeding, and more behavior appropriate to the neonate's needs and rhythms.

The task of explaining these findings is complicated by the fact that about 20 percent of the mothers changed their feeding modes between day 2 or 3 and day 28: 5 shifted from bottle to breast and 14 shifted from breast to bottle. Assuming that no artifact is responsible for the relationships between fathers' behavior patterns and initial feeding mode, how can we account for the finding that fathers of breast-fed neonates show the positively valued behavior patterns listed above and fathers of bottle-fed neonates show negatively valued behavior patterns? The proximal cause accounting for the results very likely is not the initial mode of feeding in itself but rather personal value and lifestyle factors shared by both parents that are associated differentially with the two feeding modes.

In the same vein, the fact that CSD fathers were rated reliably higher on satisfaction with their infants' personality does not imply unquestionably that the physical and social contact during the first postpartum hour was the proximal cause of the difference. There are surely efficient causal variables correlated with and underlying fatherhood and motherhood and bottle- or breast-feeding of CSD offspring, into which the variables used in this study would collapse, that would represent the proximal causal variables operating. It remains for subsequent research to clarify this matter.

Parental Behavior Outcomes

A MANCOVA of parents' behavior to their infants required that initial feed mode (bottle versus breast), final feed mode (bottle versus breast), and post-delivery medication be held constant as covariates, yielding three reliable interaction effects that were further subjected to separate univariate analyses, two involving touch and one involving smiles. The first interaction effect (figure 13) was due to a pattern in which, from 2 or 3 to 28 days, mean 10-second units of kissing of the neonates decreased for the VD mothers but increased for the CSD mothers; mean fingering of the neonates decreased for VD mothers and decreased even more for CSD mothers; and mean palming of the neonates increased for VD mothers while decreasing for CSD mothers. The second interaction effect (figure 14) reflected a mean frequency pattern involving one touch and one distal response: frequencies of palming of neonates were lower during the nonfeed observation and rose to a higher level during feeding for the short-initial-contact-duration mothers than for the long-initial-contact-duration

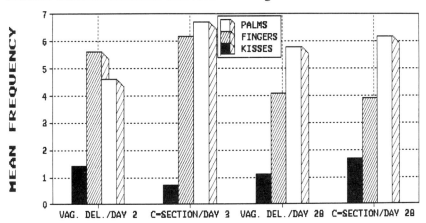

Figure 13. Maternal behavior outcomes: Kisses, fingers, and palms neonate, by observation day (2 or 3 versus 28) and delivery mode (vaginal delivery versus cesarean section).

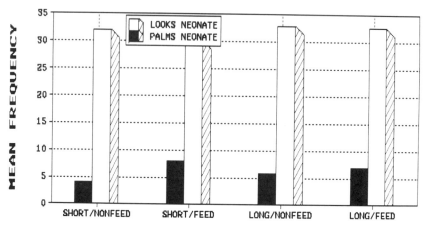

Figure 14. Maternal behavior outcomes: Palms and looks at neonate, by
feed and nonfeed interaction and contact duration (long versus
short) during the first postpartum hour.

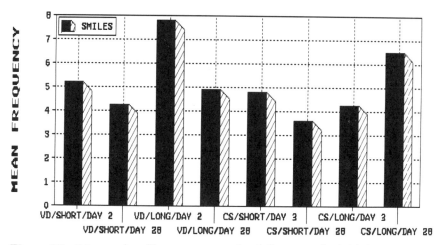

Figure 15. Maternal smiling to neonate, by delivery mode, initial contact
duration, and day of observation.

mothers; and the distal looks-at-neonate scores declined less from
feed to nonfeed observation contexts for long- than for short-initial-
contact-duration mothers. Finally, the third interaction effect (figure
15) reflected the fact that distal smiles-to-the-neonate scores declined
for short-contact-duration VD and CSD mothers and for the long-
contact-duration VD mothers and increased for the long-contact-
duration CSD mothers.

A notable result from separate CSD observations of mothers and fathers interacting with their neonates in the nonfeed setting at 3 and 28 days postpartum was the *lack* of differences found by MANCOVA on their behaviors to the infant. Nor, in a separate analysis, were differences found by MANCOVA between neonate behaviors in the presence of mother and those in presence of father. These observations thus did not support the finding that CSD fathers were more satisfied with their babies' personality than were CSD mothers.

Thus, this investigation, mounted to contribute to a research area that has been yielding both provocative and equivocal results, has provided both provocative and equivocal patterns of findings. No simple pattern of differences in outcome emerged, but the analysis provided some support for the assumption that parent physical contact and touching behaviors, such as palming, fingering, and kissing the neonate, as well as such comparable distal behaviors as smiling at and looking at the neonate, actually function as differential outcomes of the earlier experience of providing different amounts of contact and touch to the neonate during the first postpartum hour. Interesting leads for subsequent investigation have been provided by some of the results.

Parent-Infant Behavior and Learning

What might be the behavioral mechanisms that are in operation in the interchanges between infant and parent behaviors seen here? Learning processes, in particular those of operant/instrumental learning, have been shown to operate in parent-infant behavioral interchange, concurrently affecting the conditioning of both parent and infant behavior (Gewirtz, 1969, 1977, in press). From the infant's vantage, physical-contact stimuli including touch and visual and auditory stimuli can foster infant behavioral development, including social relations, to the extent that they can come to cue diverse neonate responses and to be provided contingent on these responses (as reinforcers). When provided contingently, behavior-provided stimuli like touches could function as reinforcing stimuli to condition or train neonate behaviors to the maternal cues that precede or are associated with them. It is known that touch and/or stimuli provided by physical contact, alone or together with other behavior-provided events, potentially can function as potent reinforcers for a variety of infant responses (see, for example, Etzel & Gewirtz, 1967; Gewirtz &

Pelaez-Nogueras, 1987, 1989; Rheingold, Gewirtz, & Ross, 1959). In an identical fashion, behavior-provided touches and other proximal and distal nonsocial and social events could come to cue and reinforce (that is, condition) a variety of parent responses (Gewirtz & Boyd, 1977). Hence, it is likely that contingencies for neonate and infant responses that involve touch and more distal forms of stimulation are implicated in a most important way in parent-infant interchange and the learning processes to which they contribute. Such behavior mechanisms are among those that very likely mediate between touch, physical contact, visual and auditory stimuli, and the behaviors of the neonate. Moreover, the acquisition and control mechanisms described could constitute the bases of both infant-to-parent and parent-to-infant bonding and attachment (Gewirtz, 1961).

DISCUSSION

The finding that the fathers of neonates delivered by cesarean section were rated as more satisfied than mothers with their infants 28 days later was discussed by several participants. Dr. Major wondered if there were any evidence that fathers in general report greater satisfaction than mothers at that point. In her view, the difference in responsibility for the care of the infant would have a great deal to do with the difference in satisfaction. The fathers are not as deeply involved with the day-to-day care; the mothers are the ones tending to the infant's needs, getting up at night, and so on. Dr. Gewirtz objected that some of the CSD mothers were in poor condition for some time after the delivery and the fathers may well have had to take on much extra responsibility. Dr. Field added that when the father is involved and has a real role instead of being left out, he feels much better about his child. That would not account for his feeling better about the child than the mother does, however, Dr. Major felt; it's the difference between mothers and fathers that's striking. In her opinion, a father-mother "mate effect" is operating here. Dr. Brazelton speculated that the one or two variables that this research looked at might be more appropriate for the father than for the mother and for what she sees as her total relationship with the baby.

Dr. Brazelton reported that when he has shared the neonatal assessment with fathers on the third day postpartum, at 30 days the father is not only more satisfied with the baby but significantly more sensitive to all the baby's behavior. In one study, the assessment was shared with unwed teenage fathers in Washington. In every case the father who was included actively in this way was more sensitive a month later to the baby's behavior and felt more involved. Moreover, at one year the father was significantly more attached to the baby and to the mother, and also to the system, coming in more often for medical visits, for example.

In another study reported by Dr. Kennell, Juan Keller compared a group of fathers who had routine access to their babies in the first few days and an experimental group who had an extra two hours on two occasions, during which the father gave the baby a bottle. He found significant differences six weeks later: the fathers in the experimental group looked at and talked with the baby more and were more involved with the care of the baby. He also used a self-esteem measure and found that the fathers with the extra early contact had better opinions of their own abilities as fathers.

Self-esteem was also measured in a study mentioned by Dr. Tronick that found cesarean section to be related to maternal self-esteem. The best predictor of maternal self-esteem, however, was infant outcome. If the infant was healthy, whether or not the mother had had a cesarean, maternal self-esteem was high, but if the infant was unhealthy self-esteem was low, and even lower if the delivery had been by cesarean section.

IMPACT OF INFANT MASSAGE ON THE NEONATE AND THE PARENT-INFANT RELATIONSHIP

Laurie Evans, M.A.

Infant massage has been practiced in many cultures for thousands of years (see, for example, Landers, this volume). In 1973, while visiting an orphanage in northern India, Vimala Schneider McClure watched the babies being massaged by a 12-year-old. She did not then know that she was witnessing an ancient tradition, but she recognized that the children, despite their apparent disadvantages, were loving, well adjusted, and secure. On her return to the United States, she gathered extensive information that convinced her of the vital importance of touch to development and well-being. She developed a program of infant massage and founded the International Association of Infant Massage Instructors (I.A.I.M.I.), an organization dedicated to training parents in infant massage (McClure, 1989; Schneider, 1988). This paper, by an I.A.I.M.I. instructor trainer, describes the program and its benefits for both infants and parents.

Structure of the I.A.I.M.I. Program

I.A.I.M.I. instructors offer in-services for professionals, train professionals to become instructors, and teach parents the techniques. The purpose of the infant massage program is to enhance the loving relationship between parents and infant or to help them establish this connection when it is lacking. The parent instruction is done in a series of sessions, usually five. A class setting is preferred, because it allows parents to learn from each other. All family members — mothers, fathers, and siblings — are invited to attend, and occasionally grandparents, other relatives, and babysitters participate. Instruction is offered in a variety of locations: YMCAs, churches, day care centers, high schools, hospitals, doctors' offices, social service agencies, and homes. Parents interact with their own child as the instructor role-models techniques and responses, using a doll.

Nature of the Massage

The infant massage involves both gentle tactile stimulation and loving verbal communication. It includes elements of Swedish massage, Indian massage, and reflexology, as well as original techniques for relief of colic, stroking and touch/relaxation (see figure 16). It is rhythmic and can be made soothing or stimulating, depending on the child's needs. Pressure varies according to the child's age and health.

Equally important as the techniques employed is the attitude that is

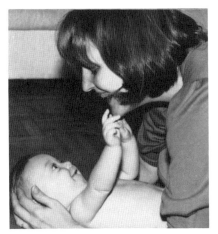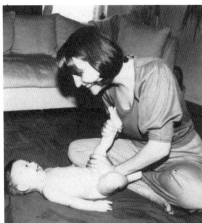

Figure 16. Laurie Evans massaging her 3 1/2-month-old daughter, Stephanie
Mear. *(left)* Getting started: Circles in the hair let the baby know
the massage is about to begin. *(right)* Swedish milking technique
increases circulation in the legs.

brought to the interaction. Massage is done *with* the baby, not *to* the
baby. Before beginning the massage, the parent seeks the baby's
permission, and the massage continues only as long as the baby
remains receptive. Throughout the entire session the parent attends
closely to the baby's responses and fully respects the baby's physical
boundaries. For example, when a baby's arms are crossed at the chest,
they are never forced open. But neither do parents give up. If an infant
avoids eye contact or resists touch, the parent works with the child at
the child's own pace.

Preparation for the massage is important. A time is set aside when
the massage can continue uninterrupted. Before the massage begins,
the parent does stretches or exercises to relax and uses visualizations
to become focused on the baby.

After asking if the baby wants a massage and determining that the
baby is receptive, the parent begins a series of rhythmic strokes, using
a cold-pressed edible oil on the hands. The baby's legs and feet are
massaged first. Newborns are less vulnerable and more receptive to
the massage in this area, and beginning here gives them a chance to get
accustomed to the massage before other areas are touched. The
massage then proceeds to the abdomen, chest, arms and hands, face,
and back. For infants under one year of age, passive exercises are done
as well.

The strokes are taught in a specific sequence, which facilitates learning by the parents and also allows the baby to feel safe with the massage. Flexibility is stressed, however, and adaptation is made whenever necessary. If a baby is hypersensitive, only one body area may be massaged during a single session. If a baby fusses at a certain point in the sequence, it must be determined if the length of the massage or sensitivity in one area of the body is the cause; experimenting with the duration and sequence is helpful. With an active, crawling baby, massage may be structured by the body area that is within reach.

Massage can begin soon after birth and can be done with older children as well. Older children have times when they need extra nurturing and attention, and touch/relaxation works beautifully at a time of stress, such as during a painful visit to the dentist or when a child starts at a new school. If the older child has not been massaged as an infant, the massage can begin in one area related to tight muscles, perhaps from sports. Then, as the child and parent become more comfortable with it, they can include other areas of the body.

The Benefits of Massage

Information on the benefits of infant massage has come from instructors' observations, parents' comments, and feedback from professionals whose clients are doing it with their children. To date there has been little formal research, but I.A.I.M.I. and its instructors welcome opportunities to study specific populations of children themselves or to work with others in incorporating I.A.I.M.I. techniques in their research.

For the infant, massage provides both stimulation and relaxation. Physically, it stimulates respiration, circulation, digestion, and elimination. Infants who are massaged often sleep more soundly. Massage relieves gas and colic, and it can aid in healing during illness by easing congestion and pain. The infant also learns to distinguish painful touch from loving touch.

Emotionally, it helps the infant to be in touch with his own body and to deal constructively with stress. He learns to feel positive about his body and worthy of being loved. He is allowed to express his feelings and learns that someone will listen.

Massage can help the infant release tension, pain, hurt, and grief.

When infants use crying as a release, their cries are listened to and supported instead of suppressed. In one such episode, Vimala Schneider McClure was doing a demonstration with a five-month-old baby whose mother massaged her regularly. The mother said that her daughter enjoyed the massage but could not tolerate having her chest touched. McClure asked the mother if the baby had had any trauma to the chest. She learned that the baby had been born two months prematurely and while hospitalized had had an injury to the skin that caused some scarring.

During the massage, the baby showed enjoyment at having her legs, feet, and abdomen massaged. When McClure began to stroke her chest, however, the baby cried. Instead of avoiding the chest or quieting the baby, McClure took a deep breath, looked the baby in the eye, and said, "You had a lot of pain. You were so brave. I am listening. Tell me about it."

The baby responded with intense crying. McClure then said, "When you're ready to let go, we'll support you through this. Your mother loves you very much."

The baby looked at McClure intensely while McClure gently massaged her chest. The cries subsided, and the mother picked her up to comfort her.

The next day, when McClure began to massage the baby's chest, the baby opened her arms and smiled. In a follow-up conversation, the mother reported that the baby continued to enjoy the entire massage. Once the release occurs, the change is permanent, although depending on the trauma and the baby's prior experience with touch, it may take more than one session for the infant to release all the tension and pain.

Parents also benefit greatly from the massage experience. They become better acquainted with the special, unique features of their baby's personality. The interaction helps them to learn the baby's body language and prepares them to become aware of any deviation from normal body functions. By increasing sensitivity and awareness, it enhances nonverbal communication. Thus massage increases both the parents' skills and their confidence in handling the baby. For the father in particular, it provides more nurturing contact and communication with the baby. When massage is practiced on a regular basis, it enhances the parent/child relationship, because it incorporates the elements necessary for bonding: eye-to-eye contact, touch, odor, verbal communication, and biorhythmicity.

Older siblings who massage a baby brother or sister feel less hostile and more accepting of the infant. They feel included in the care and take pride in being able to do something the little one really enjoys. Similarly, grandparents who feel awkward and unsure gain confidence and develop a loving relationship with their grandchild.

Some Special Situations

There are situations in which massage has benefits in addition to those seen in healthy children and healthy parent-infant relationships. Several examples follow.

Colic. Colic is frustrating, because the parent often feels helpless, exhausted, and irritated by the constant crying. A special technique for colic has been developed, to be used twice a day, and babies, instructors, and parents agree that it works. Dr. Jerry Rubin, at Rose Medical Center in Denver, over a three-year period referred parents with colicky infants to Vimala Schneider McClure, who worked with them individually. He reported an 80 to 100 percent resolution of symptoms soon after massage was begun (personal communication, 1989).

Blindness. Blind babies have no visual perception of their posture in relationship to their environment. Massage helps them to define their physical boundaries. In research with children and young adults (ages birth to 21) who are both blind and deaf, Guyer found that six months after the initiation of massage, which was given to each subject in an individualized program at least three times a week, mean time sleeping increased 19 percent and mean vocalization, verbalization, and signing increased 69 percent (New York State Department of Education, 1988). In the parent/infant relationship with a blind child, massage facilitates bonding in the absence of eye-to-eye contact, normally vital in bonding, and helps the parents to accept the child.

Cesarean section. The baby delivered by cesarean section is deprived of the tactile stimulation received during a normal birth and may be less alert because of drugs. The mother and infant may not be together for a while. The mother is in pain and often feels inadequate and hostile, and the father may feel guilty or disappointed. Massage brings the parents and baby together and helps them to release their negative feelings.

Teenage parents. Teenage parents are usually unprepared for parenting because they are still involved in growing up, and often adults judge them negatively. Massage increases a teenage parent's confidence, acceptance, and self-esteem.

Parents who do not feel connected to their babies. Some parents do not have a strong attachment to their babies. A birth with complications can lead to physical or, if mother or baby is drugged, to emotional separation. Some parents have not been nurtured themselves and may lack confidence and motivation. When they receive support and caring in class and watch other parents interact lovingly with their babies, they begin to imitate this gentle, loving behavior. They gain in confidence and in the desire to interact.

Abusive parents. Work with abusive parents should be done only by a very experienced instructor and the parents should be followed carefully and over a longer period of time than the usual five-week course. These parents are often depressed and may express boredom and hostility to the instructor. They benefit from seeing the instructor role model a loving way to be with their babies. When negative feelings are understood and even accepted, they can more readily change. Frequent praise for whatever positive interaction the parents have with the baby is very helpful.

Adoptive parents. Adoptive parents have not had the prebirth attachment to the baby, and the mother has not had the hormonal secretions. The massage helps to create a strong bond between the new parents and the baby; they begin to know they belong together.

Traumatized Infants

Another set of special situations involves infants who have experienced some form of trauma. Massage can help such infants release their tension and pain. Usually these babies avoid eye contact at first; they may cry when they are massaged. The pain and grief are often held in the chest, and the baby may protect this area by crossing the arms over the chest. When the release occurs, there is intense eye contact, the arms open, and instead of crying the infant smiles or coos. Muscles that once were rigid become flexible and supple. Where there was withdrawal and avoidance there is now trust and acceptance. These changes can be seen in situations such as the following.

Orphans and adopted babies. Infants separated from their birth mothers carry grief in their bodies. Usually it is the heart area that stores the trauma. Massaging in this area allows the release to occur.

Battered infants placed with foster families. Babies who have been abused can benefit tremendously from touch/relaxation and from being helped to release their pain. Some people question the value of encouraging the release when some of these babies will be returned to their parents. Working through the trauma is valuable in giving the infants a new frame of reference, however, and teaches them how to feel comfort and security, which are empowering.

Hospitalized infants. The needles and probes have taught these babies to associate touch with pain; they need to know that touch can be loving and sensitive. It is of utmost importance to follow their cues and to proceed only when they are willing.

Premature infants. These infants have had less experience of the warmth and comfort of the womb. They are subjected to painful intrusions, constant light, and noise. They need to learn, from the very beginning, that touch and human interaction can be enjoyable and loving. We owe it to them to give them the experience of loving, positive, soothing touch from day one.

Once parents learn the techniques, there becomes a magic in the massage. Eye contact is intense, and love flows freely. During the interaction, both baby and parent are absorbed in the process and in each other. Something happens, something changes that is hard to convey in words, but the joy and tenderness are felt by both participants and observers.

DISCUSSION

What is it about the massage that produces the results that have been described? Ms. Evans noted that so many elements go into the experience that it will be very hard for research to pinpoint just what is having the impact. Dr. Kennell offered the speculation that one component of the massage effect might be the rhythmic movement that helps the child learn how to control his or her own state. Respect for the child's signals might also contribute to that, Dr. Brazelton offered. He was impressed by the fact that the I.A.I.M.I. method advocates using only one modality at a time with hypersensitive babies, such as those who are preterm or small for gestational age. Such infants are easily overloaded, and if they are picked up, looked at, and talked to they respond by arching, pulling away, spitting up, and other indications that they are overloaded. When parents are taught to recognize signs of overloading and adapt to them by using a single modality at a time—looking *or* talking *or* touch—the infant soon shows positive responses.

Dr. Reite noted that the impact of the massage is on the entire relationship between parent and infant, however, and wondered whether in fact one could structure an experiment that would separate out the tactile from the other potent forms of communication, both verbal and nonverbal. Dr. Brazelton agreed that it would be very hard to determine whether the effect was on the baby or on the adult, and perhaps that is not the issue but rather how one affects the total.

The possibility that the massage program might lead to sexual abuse was brought up. Dr. Heidt pointed out that as with therapeutic touch, intent to help is intrinsic to the massage program, but Ms. Tribotti felt that there is a risk of people coming to the program with sexual intent and that instructors should be aware of that possibility. Dr. Brazelton speculated that the massage instruction might help to objectify such intentions for parents who have a hard time with boundaries and help them to handle their feelings differently. Ms. Evans pointed out that such parents are already so at risk that the training can hardly do more harm. Parents diaper and bathe their infants anyway, and the program provides them with a positive, loving role model. "We must not withdraw because of fear," she stressed.

Dr. Kennell agreed that such modeling can help parents avoid both sexual and nonsexual physical abuse. He commented from his own experience on the difference between North American stiffness and reluctance to touch and the attitude he encountered in Central America, where touch is used more freely among adults to comfort, soothe, and appease anger. If parents can learn this approach, he felt, they might find ways of using positive touch to avoid physical abuse.

Ms. Evans concluded by noting that right now some people are avoiding touch altogether because abuse has received so much attention. We need to learn to use touch in a healthy way and to show that part of our sensuality and our being.

EFFECTS OF GENTLE TOUCH ON THE PREMATURE INFANT

Sandra J. Tribotti, M.N., R.N.C.

The challenges of providing appropriate extrauterine environments for the premature infant are growing as we learn more about the extreme sensitivity of the infants to their environments and as the viability of the extremely immature group increases. A number of studies have been done exploring the hoped-for benefits of providing gentle touch both during and immediately following hospitalization (Field et al., 1986; Jay, 1982; Kattwinkle et al., 1975; Kramer et al., 1975; Rausch, 1981a; Rice, 1979; Scarr-Salapatek & Williams, 1973). Results in most cases are promising.

At the same time, the original work of Long, Philip, and Lucey (1980) warning of iatrogenically induced hypoxemia with excessive handling continues to ring a note of caution for clinical practice. As infants who are more and more immature populate the intensive care nursery, notes on incubators reading "Caution! Minimal Handling" proliferate. Even the findings of the above-mentioned research encourage a cautious approach to the seemingly benign and natural intervention of gentle touch for the premature infant. In two of these

(Jay, 1982; Kattwinkle et al., 1975), an occasional infant experienced increased apnea with gentle touch. Gorski and his colleagues (1983) also noted one infant to be extremely sensitive to touch.

In the study reported here, four premature infants who were medically stable were provided a gentle touch experience on three occasions within a three-day period. The investigator placed one hand on the top of the baby's head, following the natural curve of the head, and the other hand on the baby's back. Both hands were kept as still as possible throughout the intervention period. Data were collected during a preintervention phase, an intervention phase, and a postintervention phase, each 15 minutes in length. Three measures were taken: transcutaneously measured partial pressure of oxygen ($TcPO_2$) levels, respiratory regularity, and motoric activity. While some patterns could be seen across the group, the individual patterns of response of the four infants were perhaps more revealing, suggesting the possible interaction of touch effects with other variables.

Group Response to Gentle Touch

Results of the study of the four infants taken as a group are shown in figure 17. During the first session, the infants responded to gentle touch with a decrease in $TcPO_2$. This finding is perhaps not surprising, given the overwhelming predominance of nonsocial, nongentle touch experienced by the majority of infants during their intensive care nursery hospitalization (Blackburn & Barnard, 1985). During this same session, there was an increase in respiratory regularity and a slight decrease in motoric activity, giving the appearance of a "stilling" or alerting much like that seen in term infants in response to a new stimulus.

During the second session, the group demonstrated no change in $TcPO_2$ level from preintervention through intervention, and in the third session there was a slight increase in $TcPO_2$. In these sessions, regularity of respirations increased and motoric activity decreased more dramatically.

Did the infants learn over the period of the three days that this particular touch was safe and perhaps even comforting? A clue may be found in the individual responses to the touch caregiving.

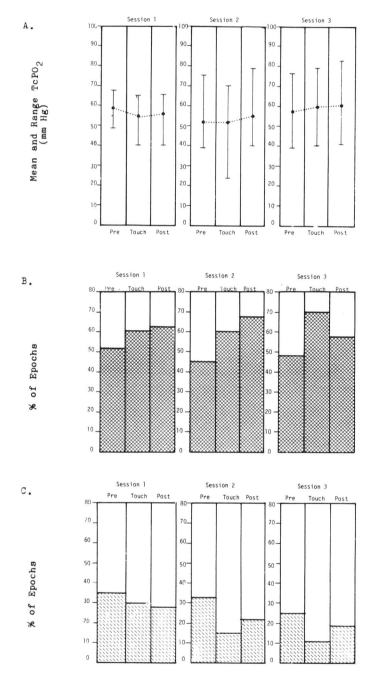

Figure 17. Group data: Preintervention, touch, and postintervention data for three sessions on (A) transcutaneus PO$_2$ (mean and range in mm/Hg), (B) regularity of respiration (percent of epochs), and (C) activity level (percent of epochs).

Individual Responses

The infants differed in the severity of initial illness, gestational age at birth, and patterns of parental visitation. Gestational age at the time of the study was between 32 and 35 weeks.

Subject number 1 was the only infant who did not match the group response of an initial drop in $TcPO_2$ (see figure 18). She was studied at 35 and 36 days of extrauterine age. In the first experience of the investigator's hands, this infant maintained her $TcPO_2$, increased her regularity of respirations, and decreased her activity. In the second and third sessions, there was an increase in $TcPO_2$ and a very remark-

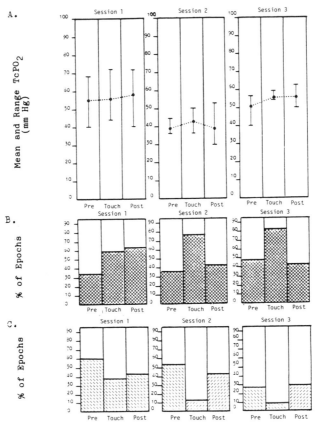

Figure 18. Individual data, subject 1: Preintervention, touch, and postintervention data for three sessions on (A) transcutaneous PO_2, (B) regularity of respiration, and (C) activity level.

able increase in regularity of respirations and a concomitant decrease in motoric activity. Examined over the three sessions, the responses seem to indicate an ability of the infant to recognize the gentle touch as a distinct, nonaversive stimulus and to use the stimulus to facilitate organization.

This baby was born at 27 weeks' gestation, the youngest and smallest of the four infants studied. She was born by cesarean section secondary to maternal herpes and required two weeks of ventilator support. At the time of the study, she had chronic lung disease and required 22 to 24 percent supplemental oxygen to maintain marginally satisfactory blood gases.

On examination of parental visiting pattern, it was clear that gentle touch was not a new, or even an unusual, experience for this child. The parents lived very close to the nursery and visited twice daily. During these visits they took turns placing their hands on her body and speaking softly to her through the portholes. The visits usually lasted an hour.

The infant who demonstrated the greatest drop in $TcPO_2$ from preintervention to intervention in the first session (see figure 19) was similar to the infant described above in that she was studied at 34 and 37 days of age and was less than 30 weeks' gestation at delivery. She too had required supplemental oxygen and was marginally tolerating room air. Her hospital course was complicated by apneic spells and seizure activity, the latter controlled by daily phenobarbital. During the second and third sessions, she demonstrated a very slight increase in $TcPO_2$.

This infant was the only one in the group to demonstrate a marked increase in motoric activity from preintervention to intervention, again in the first session. During the second and third sessions, there was very little change in motoric activity, which was generally at a low level throughout the day. Respiratory regularity increased somewhat during touch in sessions 2 and 3.

A remarkable difference in parental visiting pattern from subject 1 was forced by the fact that this infant's parents lived a long distance from the hospital. They were able to visit only once a week. In addition, the parents usually brought the four young siblings with them for visits and were often distracted. Touch was not a regular part of their visits.

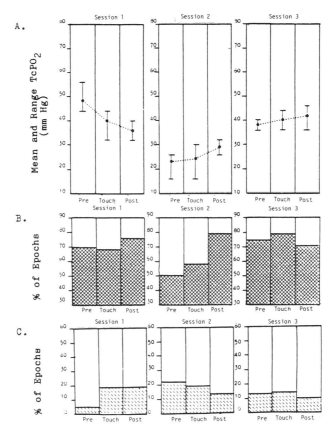

Figure 19. Individual data, subject 2: Preintervention, touch, and postintervention data for three sessions on (A) transcutaneous PO_2, (B) regularity of respiration, and (C) activity level.

Only one infant showed a decrease in $TcPO_2$ during touch in more than the first session (see figure 20). This infant was interesting in that she also demonstrated a very slight decrease in respiratory regularity and a very slight increase in motoric activity during the first touch session. In the second session, the drop in $TcPO_2$ was followed by an increase when the investigator's hands were removed in the postintervention phase. At the same time the infant showed a marked rise in respiratory regularity and a further decrease in motoric activity from an already low level.

During the third session with this infant, the pattern was more along

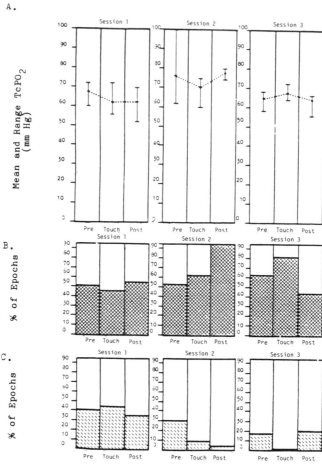

Figure 20.   Individual data, subject 3: Preintervention, touch, and postintervention data for three sessions on (A) transcutaneous PO$_2$, (B) regularity of respiration, and (C) activity level.

the expected lines, with an increase in TcPO$_2$, an increase in respiratory regularity, and a decrease in motoric activity. This was an infant who had spent only one week in the nursery, who had very mild respiratory distress, and who was 31 weeks' gestation at delivery. The mother visited daily, alone, and for brief periods of time.

The remaining infant was the most mature at delivery (34 weeks' gestation) and had a benign one-week course of hospitalization. His initial response to touch in the first session was a very minimal drop in TcPO$_2$, an increase in respiratory regularity, and a decrease in motoric

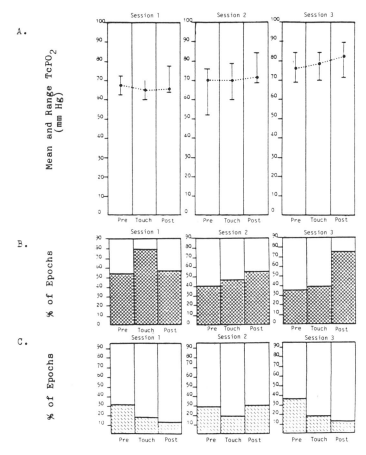

Figure 21. Individual data, subject 4: Preintervention, touch, and postintervention data for three sessions on (A) transcutaneous PO_2, (B) regularity of respiration, and (C) activity level.

activity (see figure 21). In the second session, there was no change in $TcPO_2$ level, very little change in respiratory regularity, and a small decrease in motoric activity.

In the final session, on the day following the first and second sessions, the infant showed a gradual, slight increase in $TcPO_2$ level from preintervention to touch to postintervention. Again, there was little increase in respiratory regularity and a small decrease in motoric activity. This infant was receiving phototherapy for elevated bilirubin levels and consequently wore eye patches during most of the day and night. It is difficult to know how the absence of visual stimulation may or may not have affected his response to tactile input.

The second day of the study (session 3) was the first day after discharge for this infant's mother. Until then, she had visited several times a day. His father had visited occasionally.

Touch and Containment

The recent work of Als and her colleagues (Als et al., 1986) and others encourages development of clinical skills in the observation of individual patterns of response and capability in premature infants. In response to the most natural and gentle tactile input, the infants in this study demonstrated a variety of patterns that were perhaps based on their experience of touch in their nursery experience as well as on their physiologic and developmental stability.

The touch intervention used in this study is similar to the currently utilized efforts at containment, which appears to be very effective in helping an infant, especially a very young infant, to organize himself or herself and maintain autonomic, motoric, state, and even interactional stability. Containment is often especially helpful in response to episodes of squirming (Abu-Osba et al., 1982). In my experience, it may prevent the desaturations that commonly accompany or immediately follow this motoric activity. There may also be a connection with the "range finding" described by Newman (1982).

DISCUSSION

The importance of nurses' involvement in the care of infants in neonatal intensive and intermediate care units was discussed from several perspectives. The number of different individuals who give care to an infant is extremely high, even in nurseries where each baby is assigned a primary care nurse. In an informal study of several hospital nurseries, Ms. Tribotti found that up to 42 different nurses provided nursing care for an infant over a 14-day period, in addition to physicians, physical/occupational therapists, respiratory therapists, and x-ray technicians. Dr. Kennell noted that in many cases where babies have had a very difficult course, with many caregivers, and have been thought to be retarded, having an individual caregiver for several hours a day every day can bring out the true abilities of the baby.

Dr. Brazelton reminded the group that nurses should be instructed to watch a baby for some time after an intrusive therapeutic intervention. He also described a system that has helped to develop in nurses a greater sense of involvement in each infant's development. Nurses keep records for each infant on a four-part system of behavioral development, to be handed to the next primary nurse coming on duty. They note where the infant is in motor development, state changes, autonomic regulation, and attention, the baby's response to incoming sensory stimuli. Keeping these records gives the nurses a greater feeling for the individuality of the baby. Giving the nurses a sense of investment in the baby has also reduced burnout to almost zero. The nurses come to feel very proprietary about the infants in their care, and in fact in one nursery they keep track of where parents are in their development as well. Dr. Brazelton described a four-level behavioral system through which parents of premature infants go before they develop attachment to their babies. At first they talk about the baby in chemical terms; they know the $TcPO_2$ and pH better than the house officers. The second stage begins when the baby has turned a corner; the parents begin to talk about reflex behaviors. In the third stage, they talk about what he calls "humanoid behaviors," but in terms of someone else: "When somebody talks to the baby, he alerts or turns to the voice." The fourth stage has been reached when the parents begin to talk about the baby in terms of themselves: "If I go up to her, she knows me." Nurses will not discharge an infant until parents are in that fourth stage of development.

As a result of this close interest, parents know that they are being respected and that someone is paying attention to their anxiety and their attachment. Visiting by these parents has increased significantly. Dr. Kennell seconded the importance of parental visiting, citing his strong impression that babies whose mothers spend almost all day every day with them in the intermediate nursery do much better than others. At the very least, he pointed out, it keeps away some of the caregivers and provides some helpful consistency.

The problem of carrying out this type of research in the face of the response of some of the infants was brought out. The natural thing is to follow the baby's cues, and Ms. Tribotti noted that she was uncomfortable maintaining the touch when infants responded negatively. Dr. Brazelton concurred. Researchers should control for the baby's behavior and the baby's state, he believes.

THE EFFECTS OF HANDLING ON THE BEHAVIOR OF PRETERM INFANTS

Brian Healy, Ph.D.

It has been proposed that sustained organizational patterns of preterm infant state regulation are a good indicator of the infant's ability to cope with various stressors experienced in intensive care (Garbanati & Parmelee, 1987). In addition, increased organization of state patterns may be seen not only as evidence of the maturation of the central nervous system but also as an indication of recovery from various perinatal complications.

One of the aims of our research program is to document the effect that a nursing intervention may have on the organizational properties of the infant's behavior. The study reported here documented periodic fluctuations in preterm infant behavior associated with handling.

Patterns of Infant State Organization

Research in the regulation of state behavior in premature infants suggests that between 24 and 27 weeks' gestational age there is a lack of organization with regard to state changes (Dreyfus-Brisac, 1970). During this period infants appear to be in a single state, characterized by constant body movements of the extremities, which cannot be reliably classified as an awake or an alert state, and there is little or no periodic fluctuation in sleep/wake behavior. By 28 to 30 weeks of age, certain aspects of sleep states (for example, rapid eye movements) become more regular, averaging one to four periodic bursts per minute and indicating the emergence of behavioral and physiological organization.

The first indication of sustained behavioral organization, however, appears at approximately 32 weeks of gestational age. Specific patterns of sleep behavior and associated EEG tracings indicate the emergence of physiological/behavioral synchrony. Quiet sleep is associated with slow wave patterns interspersed with inactivity similar to the tracings of the full-term infant during quiet sleep. A second pattern of mixed frequencies with predominant slow wave activity has also been identified (Dreyfus-Brisac & Monod, 1975). Between 32 and 40 weeks of age, two sleep patterns distinguishable by behavioral and physiological criteria emerge: active sleep and quiet sleep. Organized states emerge as various state parameters, each with its own periodicity, become synchronized (Nijhuis et al., 1982).

Method

The subjects consisted of a sample of preterm infants hospitalized in the special care nursery. The infants' gestational age was at least 32 weeks at the time of the study. In addition, they showed no evidence of congenital anomalies, intraventricular hemorrhage, or infection.

Each infant's behavior was videotaped for an eight-hour period while the infant was in an isolette. The attending nurses were instructed to interact with the infant in their usual fashion. The videotaped recording included at least two time periods during which the attending nurse handled the infant, usually for basic custodial care.

The episodes of handling were then isolated on the videotape, and the state behavior was coded on a six-point scale developed by Brazelton (1984): (1) quiet sleep, (2) active sleep, (3) drowsiness, (4) alert inactivity, (5) active awake, and (6) crying. The state observation was initiated 30 minutes prior to the intervention and continued during intervention (which lasted about 15 minutes) and for 30 minutes following the intervention. The state behavior was documented once every 15 seconds during the pre- and posthandling periods. Thus, a 120-point time series was produced for each period.

Each time series was first examined for the existence of trends; if any trend was detected, it was removed by detrending methods to create a stationary time series. Autoregressive integrated moving average procedures (ARIMA; Box & Jenkins, 1968) and spectral analysis were then used to identify patterns of state behavior and the frequency of state patterning — the time it takes to complete one cycle — as well as the strength of the cycle.

Results and Discussion

When the effects of handling on the behavior of preterm infants are studied, it is customary to determine how the handling procedure affects the sleep/wake pattern of the infant. Figures 22 and 23 represent such findings; they display a breakdown of the time that one of our subjects, during two separate periods on two separate days, spent in four states 30 minutes prior to a nursing intervention, during the handling episode, and 30 minutes following the episode (states 5 and 6 did not occur with sufficient frequency to make them useful measures).

Although the graphs give a good indication of how the intervention affects behavior, they give no evidence of the temporal and organizational properties of behavior change. Spectral analysis of the pre- and posthandling time series of the infant's state behavior, however, indicates that the infant tends to show a very slow, or nondeterministic, sleep/wake cycle (that is, the sleep/wake cycle cannot be described as occurring at one particular frequency) during both the pre- and postintervention periods. The analysis also indicates that there is a strong relationship between the morning and afternoon response to the intervention on both day 1 and day 2. This consistency in the infant's response to the intervention may be associated with medical status or gestational age. It is also possible that response stability may be related to the infant's ability to tolerate various interventions.

In sum, the use of spectral analysis of preterm infant behavior prior to and following a nursing intervention (or any type of intervention) may provide us with a more detailed account of the effect that this perturbation may have on the organizational properties of state behavior and be a useful technique in assessing the infant's ability to tolerate various medical procedures.

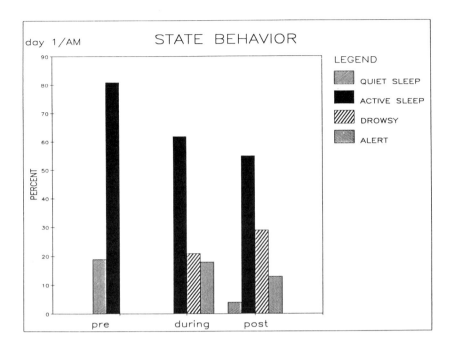

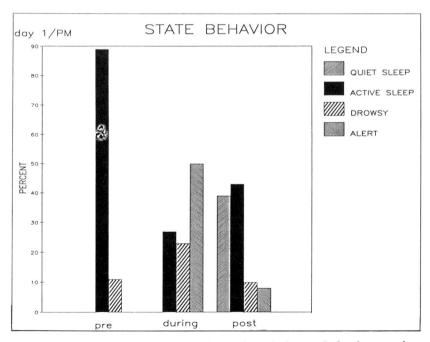

Figure 22. State behavior in one subject before, during, and after intervention, in two observations on day 1.

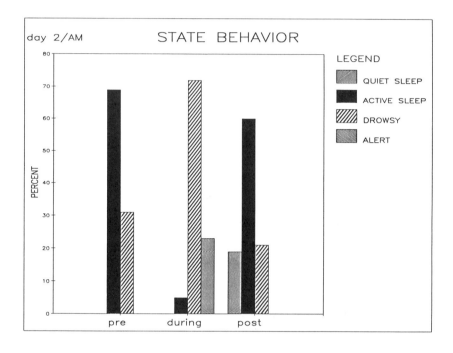

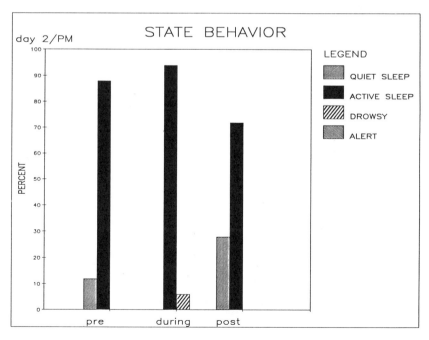

Figure 23. State behavior in same subject before, during, and after intervention, in two observations on day 2.

DISCUSSION

Dr. Field noted the similarity between Dr. Healy's findings and her own findings that $TcPO_2$ in premature infants rises following both invasive procedures and massage. This identical response to negative and positive experiences is not what one would intuitively expect, and the suggestion that handling helps infants to organize their behavior may help to explain it. $TcPO_2$ rises during quiet sleep, Dr. Brazelton commented. It is possible that the infant withdraws into quiet sleep to conserve energy. Dr. Brazelton added that learning may enter in, that over time babies may learn to use stimuli as a way of organizing themselves.

Several participants questioned whether greater organization is necessarily a positive outcome. Dr. Brazelton affirmed that among normal newborns the best predictors to future function are organization of state, range of state, and use of state, and Dr. Tronick concurred, emphasizing that coherence in state organization is desirable at this age. He suggested, however, that a longer period of observation pre- and posthandling might reveal that the unit of cycling is larger than the time sample studied so far. He also noted that differences in the point in the cycle at which the handling occurs would introduce variability in the results.

The question was raised whether the time spent in the various states was a predictor of later outcomes, and Dr. Field cited recent research by Sigman and Parmelee suggesting an inverse relationship between active sleep in newborn premature infants and 12-year IQ. Does that mean that infants in active sleep should be handled on a regular schedule to get them into other states? Maturation is more important to quiet sleep than input from the outside, Dr. Brazelton stressed, but some kinds of stimuli may increase the capacity of a baby to handle the maturational process toward quiet sleep.

MASSAGE ALTERS GROWTH AND CATECHOLAMINE PRODUCTION IN PRETERM NEWBORNS*

Tiffany M. Field, Ph.D.,
and Saul M. Schanberg, M.D.

In the last few decades, a number of investigators have studied the effects of tactile and kinesthetic stimulation on the preterm neonate (Barnard & Bee, 1983; Field et al., 1986; Friedman, Boverman, & Friedman, 1966; Hasselmayer, 1964; Rausch, 1981b; Solkoff & Matuszak, 1975; White & Labarba, 1976). Generally these types of stimulation have facilitated the subsequent growth and development of the infant, but the underlying mechanism through which these positive effects occur is unknown.

In earlier studies (Field et al., 1986; Scafidi et al., 1986), we found that a tactile/kinesthetic intervention with a group of preterm neonates over a ten-day period had the following results: (1) the stimulated infants averaged 47 percent greater weight gain per day than a control group, even though the groups did not differ in average intake; (2) the treatment infants were awake and active a greater percentage of the behavioral observation time; (3) the stimulated infants showed more mature habituation, orientation, motor activity, and range of state behavior on the Brazelton Neonatal Behavioral Assessment Scale (NBAS); and (4) the stimulated infants were hospitalized six days less than the control infants.

These findings were difficult to interpret in that the difference in weight gain could not be accounted for either by a difference in formula intake or by a lowered activity level. Intuitively, it would seem that increased activity would lead to greater energy expenditure resulting in a lesser weight gain. In our study and at least two other

*ACKNOWLEDGMENTS The authors would like to thank the infants and mothers who participated in the studies and the researchers who assisted with data collection. This research was supported by NIMH Research Scientist Development Award #MH00331 and NIMH Basic Research Grant #MH40779 to Tiffany M. Field.

studies, however, greater weight gain was reported along with greater activity level (Scafidi et al., 1986; Scott et al., 1983; Solkoff et al., 1969). In contrast, no significant weight gain was reported in studies in which activity level was diminished in the treatment infants (Hasselmayer, 1964) or similar to that in the control infants (Barnard, 1973).

We suggested that the increased activity may have contributed to increased metabolic effficiency (see Mittelman & Valenstein, 1984; Young & Torun, 1981), which in turn could lead to increased weight gain. Our sampling of activity level had been limited, however, and was taken almost immediately following a stimulation period. Moreover, because activity level had not been assessed at the beginning of the study, there was no baseline control for initial group differences.

The present investigation, therefore, was designed to correct for these methodological weaknesses (Scafidi et al., in press). In addition, we hoped to replicate the stimulation procedure and findings of the earlier study, and to add several under-the-skin variables such as growth hormone, cortisol, and catecholamine activity that might provide more information on the relationship between tactile stimulation and weight gain.

Method

Forty preterm neonates were recruited from the intermediate care unit. All were medically stable and free of ventilatory assistance and intravenous medications or feedings; none had genetic anomalies, congenital heart malformations, gastrointestinal disturbances, or central nervous system dysfunctions. They averaged 30 weeks' gestational age, 1,176 grams birthweight, 14 days of intensive care treatment, and 1,313 grams on entry into the study. They were randomly assigned to treatment and control groups, which did not differ on any of the perinatal measures. All infants received the standard nursery care procedures. In accordance with the hospital's practice, parents were encouraged to visit, touch, hold, and feed their infants.

In addition, the treatment group received tactile/kinesthetic stimulation for three 15-minute periods during three consecutive hours every day for ten days. During the first and third 5 minutes of the session, tactile stimulation was provided; the middle phase was kinesthetic stimulation. For the tactile stimulation, the infant was placed in a prone position. The stimulator gently stroked the infant with the flats of the fingers of both hands for five 1-minute segments over each region of the infant's body, as follows:

1. Six strokes from the top of the infant's head down the side of the face to the neck and back up to the top of the head, each stroke lasting approximately 10 seconds;

2. Six 10-second strokes from the back of the neck across the shoulders and back to the neck;

3. Six 10-second strokes from the upper back down to the waist and back to the upper back;

4. Six 10-second strokes from the thigh to the foot to the thigh on both legs simultaneously;

5. Six 10-second strokes from the shoulders to the wrists and wrists to shoulders on both arms simultaneously.

For the kinesthetic phase, the infant was placed in a supine position for five 1-minute segments consisting of six passive flexion/extension motions, each lasting approximately 10 seconds. The 1-minute segments focused on different parts of the body in the following sequence: right arm, left arm, right leg, left leg, and both legs simultaneously. Throughout the procedure, gentle pressure was applied so that the infant would not experience the stimulation as tickling.

Obstetric data and postnatal complications were quantified, and a number of assessments were taken throughout the study. Clinical data included formula intake, frequency of urination and stooling, average respiration rate, heart rate and body temperature, number of apneic episodes, and number of parental visits, including those with touch, holding, and feeding. The NBAS was administered prior to and following the 10-day stimulation period.

Sleep/wake behavior was observed live for 45-minute periods and by time-lapse video for 8-hour periods on the first and last days of the treatment period. Both observations were coded according to Thoman's (1975a) criteria for sleep states (including no-rapid-eye-movement [REM] sleep, active sleep without REM, and REM sleep), drowsy, inactive alert, active alert, and crying. In addition, the observer recorded indeterminate sleep, single-limb movements, multiple-limb movements, gross body movements, head turning, facial grimaces, startles, mouthing, smiles, and clenched fists. To determine the immediate effects of stimulation on sleep/wake behavior, these behaviors were observed in the treatment infants during stimulation and no-stimulation sessions and coded in the same way.

Finally, 24-hour urine samples were collected on the first and last day of treatment, and heelsticks were performed on days 1, 5, 9, and 10 for plasma assays. Urine was assayed for norepinephrine, epinephrine, dopamine, cortisol, and creatinine. Plasma was assayed for growth hormone and cortisol.

Results

Despite similar formula and caloric intake, the treatment infants averaged a 21 percent greater daily weight gain than the control infants over the treatment period (see table 1). Moreover, the average weight gain during the stimulation period as compared with the prestudy period for the treatment group (M = 14 grams) is highly significant in contrast to the control group (M = 4 grams). Because of faster weight gain, the treatment infants were hospitalized for five days less than the control group, at a cost savings of approximately $3,000 per infant.

Although no differences were noted on the NBAS on the first day of the study, the treatment group showed superior performance on the habituation cluster following the treatment period. In addition, while no differences were noted between the groups on baseline observations of sleep/wake state and activity data, at the end of the study period the treatment group showed less time in active sleep and less facial grimacing, mouthing/yawning, and clenched fists.

A comparison of the behavior of the treatment infants during the stimulation sessions and periods of no stimulation showed that during stimulation the infants experienced more active sleep, less REM sleep, more activity (in particular, more multiple-limb movements and head turns), and fewer periods with no movement. An examination of the tactile versus the kinesthetic segment suggested that during the tactile stimulation more periods of active sleep occurred, more activ-

Table 1. Intake and Weight Gain of Treatment and Control Groups: Means and Standard Deviations

	Treatment Group		**Control Group**		
	M	**(SD)**	**M**	**(SD)**	**P**
Average daily weight gain 3 days prior to study	19.6	(10.5)	24.5	(11.1)	NS
Average daily weight gain during study	33.6	(5.4)	28.4	(5.5)	.003
Number of feedings per day	8.6	(0.7)	8.9	(1.4)	NS
Average fluid intake (cc/kg/day)	161.8	(13.2)	163.7	(8.9)	NS
Calories per kg/day	118.9	(11.4)	121.1	(14.5)	NS
Calories per ounce	21.527	(1.71)	21.475	(1.76)	NS

ity including more multiple-limb movements, head turns, and gross body movements, and fewer periods without movement.

Catecholamine levels including norepinephrine, epinephrine, and dopamine increased in both groups across the treatment period (see table 2). A greater increase, however, was noted in the treatment group for norepinephrine, epinephrine, and dopamine. Both groups showed a significant increase in urinary cortisol, with no significant difference between the groups. Creatinine per volume of weight decreased for both groups, again with no significant difference between groups. Finally, plasma levels of growth hormone decreased significantly for both groups, although plasma cortisol levels did not change. Neither of the creatinine values changed.

Table 2. Catecholamine and Hormone Changes Over the Treatment Period

	Treatment Group		Control Group	
	Day 1	Day 10	Day 1	Day 10
Urine assays				
Norepinephrine	44.2 *	66.0	48.2	53.3
Epinephrine	2.6 **	4.1	3.1	3.3
Dopamine	1175.7 **	1447.8	1235.6	1433.4
Cortisol	232.3 **	274.0	248.0 **	294.7
Creatinine/vol. wt.	9.7	7.5	7.0	6.1
Creatinine/Mg/total vol.	12.9	12.4	9.1	10.0
Plasma assays				
Growth hormone	19.5 *	14.2	22.8 *	15.4
Cortisol	41.8	38.5	32.1	32.0

* $p < .05$ for adjacent means
** $p < .01$

Implications

As in our previous study, these results suggest that massage improves the clinical course of preterm infants. The stimulated infants showed a 21 percent greater daily weight gain and were discharged five days earlier. The weight gain differential in this study was not as great as in the previous study, possibly because both groups of infants were already gaining their expected weight. Several changes had been made in routine treatment that may have contributed to improved weight gain by all the babies, including formula changes and increased amounts of stimulation in the neonatal intensive care unit, such as placing the infants in a prone rather than a supine position, covering the isolettes with blankets to reduce excessive light, and adding blanket rolls for tactile stimulation and containment of the infants. Moreover, mothers were visiting more often and providing additional stimulaton.

One possible cause of the weight gain differential is the increased activity level associated with the stimulation. The increased activity during the tactile/kinesthetic sessions may contribute to increased metabolic efficiency, which in turn could lead to increased weight gain. An alternative possibility is that stimulation of the autonomic nervous system affects absorption. Sensory stimulation of newborns has been associated with the release of gastrointestinal hormones such as gastrin and insulin (Uvnäs-Moberg et al., 1987), hormones that are important for the process of food absorption. Because these hormones are vagally controlled, we are currently monitoring vagal tone (influence of the central nervous system on the heart via the vagus nerve). Preliminary analyses of these data suggest that vagal tone is increasing during the stimulation sessions. A possible mechanism underlying the relationship between massage and weight gain is that increased catecholamine and vagal activity (see Lagercrantz & Slotkin, 1986) are stimulating the production of the food absorption hormones gastrin and insulin. This possibility would be relatively easy to assess by assaying catecholamines, monitoring vagal tone, and measuring gastrin and insulin levels in the same neonates.

Differences in sleep/wake behavior suggest that the massaged infants showed more mature sleep organization. Although active sleep increased during the stimulation sessions, because the infant was being aroused, overall there was a decrease in active sleep, which is a less mature sleep state. This finding is of particular interest in that the amount of active sleep in high-risk infants has been found to be negatively related to 12-year cognitive performance (Sigman & Parmelee, 1989). In addition, the massaged infants appeared to be less stressed than the control infants, as evidenced by less mouthing, facial grimacing, and clenched fists.

The two forms of stimulation — tactile and kinesthetic — had different immediate effects on behavior. The tactile segments were more arousing for the infant, resulting in more episodes of active sleep and greater activity. These findings are consistent with Scafidi et al. (1986) and suggest that tactile stimulation has an activating effect whereas kinesthetic stimulation has a quieting effect on the neonate. One possible reason for the quieting effect of the kinesthetic stimulation is that it involves passive movement of the limbs, thereby physically limiting the infant's spontaneous movements. The novelty of the supine position in which the infant is placed for the kinesthetic stimulation may also have a quieting effect.

m
h(
di
st
cr
1⟨
n(
su
in
th
p⟨
in
e⟨

e⟨
m
m
in
a⟨
pr
ef

beneficial touch, as he has found in training people to
assessment (NBAS).

Dr. Kennell noted that what is involved is a v
a simple intervention, and expressed an inte
parents could do the massage well, since t
lationship with the infant. Dr. Field re
now comparing infants who get the
who get it from their mothers. T
babies has had a tremendous i
follow-up visits and other i
with the babies. Dr. Br
mothers have it in th
with the baby shou
but to getting b
mother has i

Dr. Sch
echola
ute

DISCUSSION

Not all nurses, even those who are well trained, are mentally capable of administering appropriate beneficial touch over a long period of time, Dr. Schanberg cautioned. In certain cases, it was noted during the study that babies massaged by a particular nurse were being stressed and instead of gaining were losing weight. In his view, the difference lies in whether the person doing the massage is sensitive to cues of the infant. Perhaps, Dr. Fisher suggested, with all the data converging that show touch to be a positive thing, we need to pay some attention to the question of who can deliver touch that leads to positive effects. We may be giving the message that touch is invariably good, when in fact there may be a sizeable proportion of nurses and parents, trained or untrained, who give touches that lead to negative effects. Dr. Brazelton felt that it would not be difficult to differentiate those people who will and who will not be successful in delivering

use the neonatal

whole relationship, not
est in knowing how many
hey have a very different replied that the research team is
massage from her staff and those
aching the mothers to massage their
mpact on the compliance rate with clinic
dications of greater parental involvement
zelton concurred, stating his view that most
em and that the person doing the intervention
ld be sensitive not only to "getting inside the baby"
ehind the mother's defenses and modeling what the
nside her.

anberg was asked to comment on the implications of the cat-
minergic changes that occurred in the stimulated infants. In
o studies have shown that at the gestational ages of the infants in
he study the adrenal medulla, which produces epinephrine, is almost
nonfunctional, and the level of norepinephrine is considerably higher than that of epinephrine. In the last two weeks of in utero life, both levels go up, and the ratio of epinephrine to norepinephrine goes up as well. It is not known that a rise in catecholamines is better, he noted, but the fact that it represents what happens in utero seems positive. Dopamine, on the other hand, represents a renal function, so the higher dopamine levels in the stimulated infants suggest that the kidneys may be doing fractionally better.

Dr. Tronick offered another hypothesis to explain the increased weight gain in the stimulated infants. He cited the Peruvians of the altiplano, who inactivate their neonates with heavy swaddling and care for them in a way that further lowers the already low oxygen available, so that the infants sleep more and move less (Tronick, 1987). These infants show accelerated weight gains. Dr. Tronick postulated that the infants in the present study, although more active, may be sleeping better, in lower energetic states for longer durations, with resultant caloric savings. Dr. Schanberg concluded that no single chemical is responsible. "If an organism is under some stress, it organizes all its biochemistry, and all aspects of the organism come into play to save it."

REDUCTION OF INFANT CRYING BY PARENT CARRYING

Ronald G. Barr, M.A., M.D.C.M., F.R.C.P.(C.)

Carrying of infants by parents and other caregivers represents a universal component of human infant care, but the range of variability from one culture to another is wide. For example, the Kalahari San hunter-gatherers are in direct contact with their infants over 90 percent of the time during daylight hours (Konner, 1976; Lozoff & Brittenham, 1979; see also Tronick, this volume). By contrast, in our society holding and carrying other than that associated with feeding occurs for approximately two to three hours a day in the first three months of life (Hunziker & Barr, 1986). Despite the range in cultural styles, however, it is difficult to ascertain the significance of such caretaking differences from cross-cultural comparisons, because other cultural differences may contribute to potential outcomes of interest.

The studies described here investigated the effect of differences in parent caregiving — especially carrying and holding — on a specific infant behavior, crying and fussing. This behavior is of particular interest because of its theoretical importance in defining patterns of early mother-infant interaction (see, for example, Barr, Bakeman, Konner, & Adamson, 1987; Bell & Ainsworth, 1972; Gekoski, Rovee-Collier, & Carulli-Rabinowitz, 1983; Lamb & Malkin, 1986) and its practical importance in the clinical syndrome of colic (see, for example, Barr, in press; Schmitt, 1985; Wessel et al., 1954). The results demonstrate that carrying and holding behavior is a determinant of normal infant behavior during the first three months but that there are limits to its effectiveness as a regulator of infant state.

Carrying and Cry/Fuss Behavior

In Western societies, the time an infant spends crying per day tends to increase until about six weeks, declining slowly thereafter, and to cluster during the evening hours, although there is considerable variability between subjects (Brazelton, 1962; Hunziker & Barr, 1986). A considerable body of experimental literature has confirmed the effectiveness of many of the elements of carrying behavior in soothing already-crying infants (for a review, see Hunziker & Barr, 1986). We wondered whether making increased carrying a routine part of the caregiving structure might affect crying and fussing behavior. We speculated that the increased carrying would act to modulate infant state by preemptively preventing the infant from entering a crying state.

To test this hypothesis, we designed a randomized controlled trial in which the experimental ("supplemental carrying") group were asked to increase the amount of carrying and holding to a minimum of 3 hours per day; the control mothers were asked to have their infants facing a mobile or a smiling face figure when placed in their cribs. We were interested in the results related to the independent variable (holding and carrying) as well as to the dependent variable (cry/fuss behavior), for we had been able to find little or no systematic description of holding and carrying behavior in our society (Konner, 1976; Lozoff & Brittenham, 1979). During the intervention period—weeks 4 to 12 of life—the control group mothers held and carried their infants 2.7 hours per day, distributed as shown in figure 24. Of the total, .74 hours (27 percent) was done while the infant was crying or

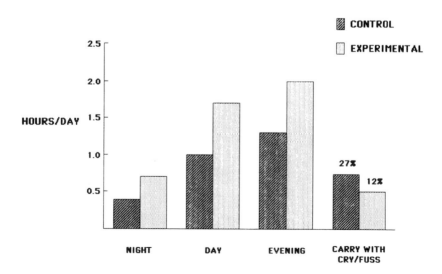

Figure 24. Duration of holding/carrying in experimental and control groups.

fussing. The experimental group mothers were asked to carry their infants a minimum of 3 hours per day and were encouraged to do the carrying throughout the day, not only in response to crying, in addition to that which occurred during feeding, and independently of whether the infant was awake or asleep. This pattern resulted in an increase in total duration of carrying and holding to 4.4 hours per day, an overall difference of 1.7 hours per day. While the amount was greater, the distribution was similar (see figure 24).

The results showed that the infants with supplemental carrying cried significantly less than the control infants throughout the period of intervention (see figure 25). The difference was greatest at the time of typical peak crying (six weeks of age), amounting to 43 percent less cry/fuss over 24 hours. The greatest effect was on duration of evening crying, which was 54 percent lower than that of the control infants at six weeks. Perhaps the most impressive finding is that not only the amount but the pattern of cry/fuss was changed. The typical six-week peak was obliterated, and cry/fuss behavior declined gradually from the end of the baseline period on. By contrast, the cry/fuss behavior in the control group demonstrated the usual pattern with the peak at six weeks.

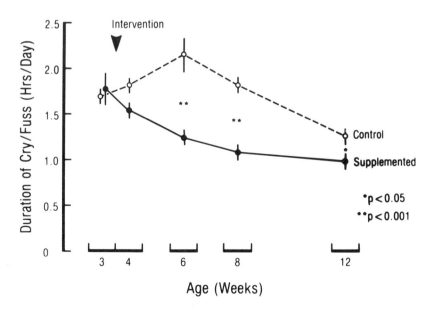

Figure 25. Duration of cry/fuss in experimental (supplemented) and control groups.

Two other comparisons were of interest. The first concerns the question of what replaced the reduced cry/fuss behavior. There were no differences in sleep or feeding duration between groups at any age, but awake-and-content behavior was significantly higher in the supplemented infants at weeks 4, 6, and 8. This finding implies that the intervention shifted arousal to a state of increased visual and auditory alertness, potentially more conducive to positive social contact. Second, there were no differences between groups in *frequency* of cry/fuss episodes; the primary overall effect was a reduction in *bout length* of episodes, suggesting that the effect of holding and carrying may be not so much to prevent infants from crying, as we had expected, but rather to diminish the likelihood that crying will be prolonged. If, as Murray (1979) has speculated, it is the prolonged, unremitting character of crying that provokes negative parental reactions, then carrying may have an important indirect role in fostering positive parent perceptions and mother-infant interaction by reducing prolonged crying bouts.

The main results raised two important questions having to do with the role of holding and carrying. The first was whether or not increased carrying and holding might have value in treating infants presenting with "colic." The second was whether, given the change not only in amount but also in pattern, the early crying and fussing peak is a behavioral universal or a function of holding and carrying (or, more generally, the structure of infant caregiving).

Carrying and Colic

Several considerations pointed to our studying the potential implications of holding and carrying for treatment of colic. Despite the apparent lack of success of nonpharmacological means of treatment in this clinical syndrome, the size of the carrying effect in normal infants made its possible application reasonable. Since the amount of carrying and holding was greater than that typical in our society, previous perceptions of the ineffectiveness of behavioral treatments might be attributable to lack of a sufficient "dose" of the behavioral interventions. A more practical rationale for studying this intervention was the almost universal assumption in lay publication reports of our carrying study that what was effective for normal infants would be effective for infants with colic, despite the fact that the data did not support — nor did the report claim — such effectiveness.

The crying of colic shows a pattern similar to that of normal children, although it is often defined by additional criteria, such as facial pain expressions, presence of gas and distension, or resistance to soothing behavior. Many people would limit the term "colic" to that amount of crying that meets Wessel's (Wessel et al., 1954) "rule of threes" — more than three hours a day for more than three days a week for more than three weeks — but otherwise the pattern across weeks, within the day, and between subjects is very similar to that of normal infants. Because of these similarities and the usual absence of underlying pathology, opinion is mixed on whether colic represents a clinical syndrome distinct from crying in normal infants or whether it represents the upper end of a spectrum of otherwise normal crying behavior (see, for example, Barr, in press).

To test the hypothesis concerning the potential role of supplemental carrying as a therapy in colic, we carried out a randomized controlled trial with a design parallel to the previous carrying study with normal infants (Barr et al., 1989). For this trial, colic was defined as crying seen as a problem by both the parents and the physician — a definition that lacks the homogeneity of a predefined amount of crying but has the advantage of being more relevant to daily pediatric practice. Following a one-week baseline period, the experimental group received standard advice plus the instruction to increase supplemental carrying — that is, carrying in addition to that which occurs in response to crying. The control group received standard advice only, which included being responsive to the infant's crying but no formula changes and no recommendations to use medications.

In comparison with the previous study in nonclinical infants, there were some interesting differences in these two- to four-week-old infants at the point of entry into the trial. On average, they were crying and fussing 3.5 hours per day by diary records, thereby meeting the first two of Wessel's (Wessel et al., 1954) criteria. Moreover, they were already being carried 4.5 hours per day, about as much as the normal infants were carried *after* the instruction to increase carrying (Hunziker & Barr, 1986). After the intervention, overall carrying of the supplemented infants with colic increased to 6.3 hours per day — 77 percent more than occurred in the control group. In marked contrast to the findings in normal infants, however, there was no improvement in duration or frequency of crying and fussing in the supplementally carried infants with colic compared with colic controls. In both groups, the crying and fussing declined monotonically following the intervention through to 12 weeks of age.

Given the rather impressive findings in the previous study of normal infants, the lack of effect of supplemental carrying and holding in this study may be somewhat surprising. Of course, the study in normal infants is not directly comparable to the colic study, and it is possible that the differences in effect were due to differences in the design of the two studies. For example, the "control" group in the colic study actually received a true intervention of standard pediatric advice (including advice to be responsive), which may have been more efficacious than is usually thought. In any case, there was clearly no additional benefit of supplemental carrying over standard advice. The study underlines the importance of testing extrapolations of findings from nonclinical infants to clinical infants presenting with colic, rather than assuming a priori that such findings will be directly applicable.

On the other hand, it is arguably the case that the differences have other implications for understanding the effect of carrying and holding on infant crying or, more broadly, on infant state. For example, this study may be defining the limits of the power of carrying and holding to modify crying in children who are already having, or who have already developed, difficulty in state control. This hypothesis is consistent with the clinical observation that these infants are "difficult to soothe" (Schmitt, 1985; Wessel et al., 1954). This study leaves unanswered, however, the question of whether, if it were part of the normal structure of caregiving *prior* to the development of colic — that is, from birth — increased carrying and holding would prevent the development of colic (or difficulty in state control).

Carrying and Holding as Part of a Caregiving "Package"

In real life, differences in carrying and holding behavior are not typically found in isolation from other structural aspects of infant caregiving. In the !Kung San hunter-gatherers, for example, almost constant carrying and holding coexists with short interfeed intervals, holding the infant upright, close proximity, and universal responsiveness to distress signals (Barr, Bakeman, Konner, & Adamson, 1987; Konner, 1976) — all features that should predispose to less crying. Indeed, both cross-cultural and cross-species comparisons suggest that these features often cluster together and may be considered typical of higher primate caregiving patterns throughout most of our evolutionary history (Blurton Jones, 1972; Konner, 1976, 1981; Lozoff & Brittenham, 1979; Plooij, 1984).

It is therefore of some interest to know whether or not the early crying peak that typifies infant behavior in Western societies is also present when this caregiving pattern is the norm. In such a context, the specific influence of holding and carrying cannot be isolated from other possible influences, but quantifiable measures of crying may give an indication of the potential maximum effectiveness of the caregiving package of which the carrying and holding is a part. In this sense, it would help to define the least amount of crying that might be achievable through caregiving practices. Arguably, it would also provide a test of whether the early crying peak is indeed a behavioral universal — one of the implications of the carrying study in normal infants.

A data set collected by Melvin Konner permitted us a first look at the pattern of infant crying in a sample of !Kung San hunter-gatherers (Barr, Konner, Bakeman, & Adamson, 1987). The data set consists of six direct 15-minute observations at different age points for a total of 68 observations on 46 infants. Using an interval time-sampling technique, researchers recorded the presence of crying or fretting by the infant for each five-second interval during the observation. A clear pattern of elevated crying and fretting behavior (in minutes per hour of observation during waking hours) in the form of an inverted U-shaped curve, very similar to that seen in Western societies, emerged from these observations. In contrast to the Western data, however, the peak occurred during the third month. Whether or not the timing of the peak is artifactual, there is little question that the elevation is unique to the first three months of life. The nature of the measures and the fact that the observations were concentrated during the daytime do not permit direct comparisons to be made of *amount* of crying and fretting, but the *pattern* is clearly similar.

These data provide fairly strong evidence that carrying and holding, even when packaged with other potentially soothing caregiving behaviors, do not eliminate the early crying peak. Moreover, they provide indirect evidence in favor of the hypothesis that this unique early crying pattern may be a behavioral universal of the species. Unfortunately, the data are insufficient to determine whether the evening clustering also occurs, nor do they make clear whether the crying and fretting can be said to occur in prolonged bouts. Nevertheless, they may provide a rough estimate of the "lower boundary" of state regulation provided by a responsive caregiving structure.

Summary

Holding and carrying, as the complex embodiment of touch in the everyday life of early mother-infant interaction, clearly have considerable power to contribute to the regulation of infant state under caregiving conditions considered typical in Western society, but this power appears to be limited at both upper and lower boundaries. In children with colic, additional carrying appears to add no therapeutic power to that provided by reassurance and responsive caregiving, and in infants exposed to constant holding and carrying plus other soothing caregiving techniques, the early crying peak still persists. By virtue of their influence on infant state, the potential relevance of holding and carrying in facilitating positive mother-infant interaction and in mediating disturbances of mother-infant relationships would seem to be worth further investigation.

DISCUSSION

Dr. Brazelton volunteered that nighttime observations in a study in Mayan Mexico demonstrated that evening fussing does go across cultures, even when babies never cry in the daytime. Just looking at daytime behavior in a carrying culture is not enough, because there may be a cycling of crying activity.

Studies of infant crying do not generally distinguish between *reflexive crying* — crying in response to pain or discomfort — and *instrumental crying* — crying used to evoke behavior from the parent. Dr. Gewirtz speculated that introducing carrying into the study might shed some light on the two kinds of crying behavior. Carrying might be eliminating or lowering the instrumental cries because it keeps the child interested. It might also be containing most of the reflexive cries because it makes the mother sensitive to pre-cry cues. He would like to see the cries separated in such a study and believes that mothers are generally able to distinguish between them. Dr. Barr was skeptical of parents' ability to distinguish reflexive and instrumental cries. He agreed with Dr. Brazelton's comment that parents can be taught about the two kinds of crying and that understanding the difference between them can make parents more responsive to their babies, but he doubted that parents could determine, for every cry, whether it was reflexive or instrumental. Studies have shown that the contextual situation has more to do with what parents actually do in response to a cry than any information transmitted by the cry itself.

Dr. Gewirtz agreed on the importance of the context. In response to a query by Dr. Oller, who is looking for behavioral clues to the distinction between reflexive and nonreflexive cries in connection with his work with infant vocalizations (e.g., Oller, 1986), Dr. Gewirtz described research of his own in which instrumental cries are identified by elimination of possible causes for reflexive cries. When cries that may be associated with the need for feeding, diapering, and so on have been eliminated, the residual cries can be manipulated as operants: if the mother's behavior is contingent on cries, they increase in incidence, and if the mother is noncontingent, cries decrease. But it is difficult to characterize the two kinds of cries separately, such as by the way the baby is acting.

PART III

DEVELOPMENTAL AND CLINICAL PERSPECTIVES

TACTILE HEARING
FOR DEAF CHILDREN

D. Kimbrough Oller, Ph.D.

Deaf children often do not learn to speak or to understand speech because lipreading and hearing aids cannot supply sufficient information about the sounds of speech to support normal vocal development. A major attempt to solve the problem of deafness in childhood is underway, utilizing the intact sense of touch as a substitute for the damaged sense of hearing. Special devices called *tactual vocoders* transmit sound to the skin of the deaf wearer, presenting patterns of stimulation that correspond systematically to particular sounds. Users learn to recognize particular sounds and eventually to match the sounds they feel with the sounds of their own voices, also felt on the skin. Even present-day tactual vocoders can provide major assistance to the deaf in speech reception and can greatly enhance the education process.

Sound Perception and the Acquisition of Language

The child who suffers from a congenital or prelinguistic hearing impairment is educationally disadvantaged. The degree of hearing loss is clearly related to the degree of disadvantage, but the effect is not linear. Most children who are mildly or moderately impaired learn to speak and to understand speech quite effectively and can function in the mainstream. A profound loss, on the other hand, usually produces a very major speech impairment and may make mainstreaming inadvisable. Between these two levels of hearing loss is an intermediate level referred to as severe. This is the level at which, in general, the shift from very impaired speech function to virtually normal function is seen (figure 26).

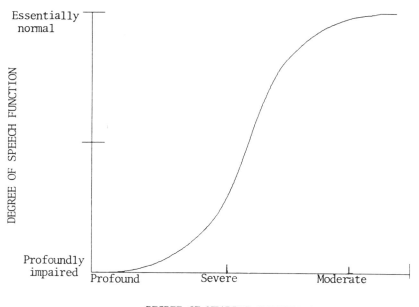

DEGREE OF HEARING IMPAIRMENT

Figure 26.   Variations in speech functions associated with different degrees of hearing impairment.

The nonlinear increase in speech function seen in children of increasing amounts of hearing suggests that learning to perceive and produce speech requires some threshold level of receptivity. A typical moderate hearing loss apparently provides access to a sufficient proportion of the phonetic code that bears the messages of language, whereas a typical profound loss does not. A severe loss may produce a good or a poor speech outcome, depending on how aggressively the problem is treated educationally.

Lipreading alone provides about 30 percent of the linguistic code (Erber, 1974). Some contrasts in speech sounds are easy to perceive visually (for example, consonants that involve the lips as opposed to the tongue), while others are impossible to see (for example, /t/ versus /d/ or /m/ versus /b/). In deaf persons whose impairment is total, lipreading is for practical purposes the only method of input. Apparently 30 percent of the phonetic code is not enough for the purposes of language acquisition; the totally deaf rarely learn spoken language.

If hearing aids are used in addition to lipreading, an additional proportion of the linguistic code can be made available. The amount is clearly dependent on the type and degree of hearing loss and other factors; it is perhaps 10 percent for the profoundly deaf who have some residual hearing, 20 percent for the severely impaired, and 30 percent for the moderately impaired. Thus the proportion of the code available with a combination of lipreading and hearing aids would be approximately 40 percent for the profoundly (but not totally) deaf, 50 percent for the severely impaired, and 60 percent for the moderately impaired.

As we have noted, moderately impaired persons usually learn effective speech communication, even though, given the estimates above, as much as 40 percent of the linguistic code is not available to them. If these estimates are correct, they suggest that if one could provide the profoundly deaf with another means of access to sounds of speech, a means that would increase the proportion of the code they could recognize by 20 percent or so, one might produce a major change in level of function. Such a change could mean the difference between the ability to function in a hearing world or not, the difference between being able to maintain gainful employment or not, the difference between being able to pay taxes or not.

Sensory Substitution with Tactual Vocoders

Over the past 12 years, we have been working on a method of sensory substitution that may, within the next decade or so, make this difference. It involves the use of tactual vocoders, which take sound through a microphone, divide it into a number of frequency bands, and use the information in each band to drive a stimulator on the skin. Stimulators can be vibrotactile or electrocutaneous, presenting painless tickle-like sensations to the skin of the user. They are generally worn in a linear array on the arm, leg, abdomen, hand, or forehead (figure 27). The person wearing a tactual vocoder feels sound in real time as a pattern of stimulation on the skin. The sound /s/ consists primarily of high frequency information and produces stimulation on the high frequency side of the array, whereas a low frequency sound such as /u/ produces stimulation on the other side. As sounds change, the points of stimulation change, yielding a systematic pattern that can be learned. The wearer's task is to learn to recognize particular sound types and associate them with particular events or sources of the sounds. For speech perception, the task is to learn to recognize that a

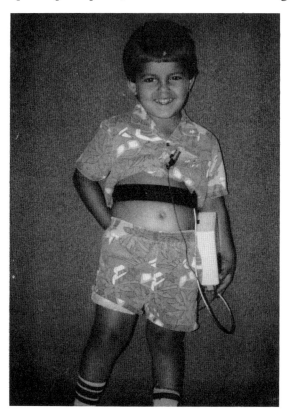

Figure 27.   Hearing-impaired child in University of Miami project wearing a 16-channel tactual vocoder by Tacticon (designed by Frank Saunders).

particular sound has a particular phonetic/phonemic value—much the same task that must be accomplished auditorily by normal listeners. For speech production, the task is to learn to produce patterns of skin stimulation that correspond to learned phonetic or phonemic patterns of parents or trainers.

In order to serve successfully as an aid to learning and to speech performance, such a device must provide acoustic/speech information that is not already available to hearing-impaired persons through lipreading or hearing aids. That information must be integrated in real-time conversation with the information provided through other modalities. The goal of our research is to provide tactile speech information in sufficient quantity to raise the available proportion of the linguistic code to the threshold level needed for the acquisition of intelligible speech. How do the current tactual vocoders and those projected in the near future measure up to these criteria? A number of researchers have addressed these issues.

1. *Can tactual vocoders provide additional information to the deaf?*

Not by design but by serendipity, the acoustic information provided by tactual vocoders tends to be complementary with that provided by lipreading and hearing aids. Early researchers (for example, Pickett & Pickett, 1963) found that certain speech contrasts that are not easily seen in lipreading because they are produced at the same place of articulation, such as /s/ and /t/, are readily discriminated by tactual vocoders (see Oller & Eilers, 1988, for a review of a variety of such contrasts). Similarly, there are many differences between the kinds of information transmitted well through hearing aids and those transmitted well through tactual vocoders. In general, for example, vocoders do better with contrasts that include high frequency information, because severe to profound hearing losses usually leave residual hearing only at low frequencies. The pattern of complementarity of information has been verified with both adults and children (see, for example, Eilers, Widen, & Oller, 1988; Sparks et al., 1978).

2. *Can tactual information be integrated with visual and auditory information in real-time speech communication?*

The early researchers in tactual vocoders soon found that recognizing sounds in an experimental situation is not the same as understanding speech in real time (see Kirman, 1973). The problem of what it would take to understand real speech was badly misjudged. The key mistake was to underestimate the amount of training necessary for a subject to acquire substantial tactual knowledge of sound. Engelmann and Rosov (1975) were the first to make a breakthrough, after training subjects in systematic vocabulary acquisition for 40 hours and more with their 24-channel vibrotactile vocoder. The subjects (mostly hearing people whose audition was masked for experimentation) learned to recognize words from a closed set at remarkable levels of accuracy. Subjects learned from one to three words per hour of training and never leveled off; they continued to learn new words for as long as they were trained, even well beyond 100 hours. The studies were replicated very effectively with deaf children as subjects.

The subjects trained in these experiments were able to recognize, through the tactual vocoder alone, sentences composed over the known vocabulary and pronounced at normal rates of articulation. The same outcome within roughly the same training format has been found in at least three other laboratories and with a variety of tactual vocoders (see, for example, Brooks & Frost, 1983; Oller & Eilers, 1988; Weisenberger & Miller, 1987).

Moreover, recent tests have demonstrated the ability of trained subjects to integrate information across sensory modalities. Two studies using a 16-channel bench-top vibrotactile vocoder (Brooks et al., 1986a, 1986b; Weisenberger & Miller, 1987) have found that subjects trained first in vocabulary acquisition and speech discrimination with the tactual vocoder can understand running speech in a lipreading-plus-vocoder condition at two to three times the rate found in a lipreading condition alone. While performance in both conditions improves with time, the difference tends to increase with time. These studies have been conducted primarily with hearing subjects, but deaf subjects have been found to show similar though not such dramatic differences (Lynch et al., 1989; Weisenberger, 1988). Work with portable electrocutaneous devices with deaf subjects also shows consistent gains in conjunction with lipreading, although the improvements are considerably smaller than with the laboratory vibrotactile devices (Lynch, et al., 1988; Weisenberger, 1988). The results suggest that substantial improvements can be made in devices that can be used as prostheses, by incorporating features of the laboratory devices. Similarly, work in our laboratories has shown the ability of deaf adults and children to integrate information from vocoders and hearing aids

(Lynch et al., 1989). These results make it clear that not only can tactual vocoders provide potentially useful information for the deaf but that the information can be integrated with other sensory information in real time in the perception of speech presented at normal rates.

3. *How much information can tactual vocoders provide?*

While we know that hearing subjects, trained with tactual vocoders for 40 to 80 hours, can track speech at twice the rate or more with the vocoder-plus-lipreading than with lipreading alone, there are a number of questions that remain unanswered. We do not know, for example, how to translate that increase in rate of tracking into an increase in code learnability for a deaf child. Does the doubled rate suggest that a doubled proportion of the speech code is available? Perhaps it does, and perhaps, if the same tactile device is used as a learning aid prosthesis, worn all the time by a deaf user, it would be possible to learn the speech code in a manner similar to a moderately hearing-impaired child who functions with a hearing aid.

It is also unclear how much improvement in the tracking rates could be achieved using different training methods or longer training. We know that long-term training is indispensable and that with a well-designed device continued training produces continued increases in performance. Thus far no one, even after hundreds of hours, has trained users to near-perfect performance on complex tasks such as open-set word recognition or speech tracking.

Finally, it is not clear how much improvement can come from advances in the devices themselves. The bulky laboratory vibrotactile devices have been far more successful than miniaturized electrocutaneous units, but a number of laboratories are attempting to develop a miniaturized vibrotactile system. A recent study using a laboratory prototype of such a system (Weisenberger, Broadstone, & Saunders, 1989) indicates that gains similar to those with the more bulky devices are most likely possible. Other major improvements in tactual vocoders may come from the development of better means of processing the signal for presentation to the skin (Ozdamar et al., 1988).

Given all the unknowns, it is hard to estimate how much speech information can be provided through tactual vocoders now and in the future. Our guess, based on laboratory and classroom research, is that the best laboratory devices can already produce a 10 to 20 percent increment in the amount of speech information available to subjects and that the best miniaturized systems can produce perhaps a 5 percent gain. Thus, for those severely impaired individuals whose hearing losses leave them just at the threshold of normal speech, the existing miniaturized systems could make a major difference. If we can succeed in miniaturizing appropriately a device with the transmission capability of the best laboratory vibrotactile systems, we should be able to see major improvements in the majority of severely impaired subjects and many profoundly impaired subjects. And with the next generation of stimulators and of signal processing, the devices may well be able to transmit double the amount of critical information and may make it possible for even the most profoundly deaf subjects to achieve speech acquisition comparable to that now obtained by the moderately impaired.

DISCUSSION

The potential of tactual vocoders for aiding learning in deaf children was of keen interest to the participants. Deaf children generally suffer a severe lag in reading skills, largely because of their lack of knowledge of phonetics and the basic structure of language. Children who have been working for some years with the units in Dr. Oller's laboratories, however — even profoundly deaf children — are reading at age level, and some of them are beyond age level in both reading and mathematics. Intelligible speech is produced consistently by children with severe hearing impairments, but much less consistently by the profoundly impaired.

Dr. Oller was asked to describe in greater detail the program he operates in collaboration with the Dade County Public Schools. The children are in a full-time eclectic training program that teaches sign language, encourages lipreading and the use of residual hearing, and includes all the academic areas. At the elementary school age, the children wear the devices for several hours a day. During 30 to 40 minutes of that time, their attention is specifically directed to recognizing patterns. This program is the largest in the world that extensively utilizes multichannel tactual vocoders; two-channel devices are in relatively widespread use in classrooms around the country.

The program also works with infants as young as six months in a parent-infant program. Work with infants is still difficult, however, because the best of the present stimulators are not entirely comfortable. Dr. Brazelton noted that lack of hearing is extremely disorganizing for infants. They get into autisms and demonstrate in all sorts of ways that they are out of control; it is a major assault to their learning. Dr. Oller agreed, expressing his conviction that for the majority of profoundly deaf children, hearing is initially the only problem; if that problem could be solved early, the other problems associated with profound deafness would never appear.

MASSAGE WITH CHILD AND ADOLESCENT PSYCHIATRIC PATIENTS*

**Sandra K. Larson, Ph.D.,
and Tiffany M. Field, Ph.D.**

Relaxation therapy (RT) has become increasingly popular as a therapeutic technique for use with psychiatric patients (Blaney, 1981). Some have noted that RT is as effective as psychotherapy and pharmacology in reducing depression and related anxiety (McLean & Hakistian, 1979); with adolescents it has proved more effective than cognitive behavior therapy (Reynolds & Coats, 1986). Typically, RT involves a variety of techniques including yoga, aerobics, massage, and progressive muscle relaxation with visual imagery.

In a recent study (Platania et al., 1989), we assessed the effects of RT sessions that included yoga, massage, and progressive muscle relaxa-

*ACKNOWLEDGMENTS The authors would like to thank the children and adolescents who participated in these studies and the researchers who assisted with data collection. This research was supported by NIMH Research Scientist Development Award #MH00331 and NIMH Basic Research Grant #MH40779 to Tiffany M. Field.

tion with visual imagery on 40 clinically diagnosed adjustment disorder and depressed children and adolescents (8 to 18 years old) who were hospitalized on a psychiatric unit. Both diagnostic groups appeared to benefit from the RT class, reporting a decrease in anxiety as well as showing a decrease in anxious behavior and an increase in activity level and positive affect. It was not clear, however, whether one of the components of the therapy or all three were contributing to the beneficial effects. Another study was therefore undertaken to try to tease apart the individual effects of these different forms of RT. Because much less is known about the effects of massage than of progressive muscle relaxation on child and adolescent psychiatric patients, and because these patients are rarely touched, we decided to look first at the effects of massage on stress alleviation.

Method

A pre- and postevaluation design was used, with subjects serving as their own controls. The subjects (N = 16 to date) were children and adolescents with diagnoses of depression or adjustment disorder, which represent the most commonly diagnosed problems on adolescent psychiatric units. They ranged in age from 8 to 16 years (M = 11 years) and were from lower to middle socioeconomic backgrounds.

The subjects received 30 minutes of Swedish massage per day for five days. The massage consisted of carefully timed stroking movements in each of three regions: up and down the neck, from the neck to the shoulders and back to the neck, and from the neck to the waist and back to the neck. The sequence lasted approximately 15 minutes and was repeated in its entirety in the 30-minute session. The massage was administered by graduate students (in physical therapy, premed, or psychology) trained in the standard massage procedure.

The assessments of the effects of the massage therapy included self-reports of anxiety (the State-Trait Anxiety Inventory for Children [STAIC, Spielberger, Gorsuch, & Lushene, 1970]) and mood levels (the Profile of Mood States [POMS, McNair, Lorr, & Droppleman, 1971]); behavior ratings by an independent examiner on seven different scales: state, affect, activity level, anxiety level, fidgety/nervous behavior, vocalization, and cooperation; activity monitoring by an actometer, or "activity watch" worn on the wrist; pulse rate; saliva samples of cortisol; time-lapse videotaping of nighttime sleep; and urine samples of cortisol and catecholamines, including norepinephrine, epinephrine, and dopamine. On the first and last days of the treatment period, the baseline, session, and follow-up assessment measures were collected according to the following schedule:

- Thirty minutes prior to the massage, STAIC and POMS taken;

- Immediately prior to the massage, saliva samples, activity level, and pulse rate taken; behavior observation ratings made based on previous 30 minutes of subject's behavior;

- Immediately after the session, activity level and pulse rate taken; behavior ratings completed based on behavior noted during the session; self-report measures again taken;

- Thirty minutes following session, saliva samples, activity level, and pulse rate again taken; behavior ratings made based on previous 30 minutes of behavior.

The subjects' therapists completed ratings based on the subject's general behavior at that time (that day or the previous day). On the first and last treatment days, nighttime sleep was videotaped and subjects were asked to collect a 24-hour urine sample.

Results

Comparisons were made between pre- and post-session data for the first day of the treatment to determine the immediate effects of the massage sessions. These were followed by comparisons between baseline values (or pre-session values) on day 1 and day 5 of the study, to determine longer-term effects.

Immediate effects. As table 3 shows, the levels of self-reported anxiety and depression diminished from pre- to post-massage; on both the STAIC and the POMS, ratings following the massage were significantly lower. Similarly, a number of changes in the behavior ratings suggested that the subjects were less anxious following the massage.

Significant differences were noted in state, activity, and vocalization ratings, suggesting that the subjects, not surprisingly, became less active during the sessions. In addition, significantly lower ratings of behavioral anxiety were made following the massage sessions. The diminution in activity level was also reflected in the activity watch readings, which were significantly lower following the sessions. Paralleling the decreased activity were decreases in heart rate following the massage. Finally, the decreases in activity and anxiety levels were reflected in lower cortisol values.

Table 3. Means for Measures, Pre- and Post-Massage, Day 1

	Pre	Post	t value
Self-report			
State anxiety (STAIC)	32.9	26.0	4.39****
Depression (POMS)	16.9	13.0	2.39*
Behavior observation scale			
State	2.4	1.6	4.96****
Affect	1.9	2.1	N.S.
Activity	1.7	1.3	N.S.
Anxiety	1.8	1.4	2.42*
Fidgeting	1.6	1.3	N.S.
Vocalization	1.9	1.3	3.47***
Cooperation	2.8	2.8	N.S.
Activity level (Actometer)	6.7	1.0	3.13**
Pulse (BPM)	88.8	79.0	4.06****
Cortisol (ng/ml)	1.0	.7	2.27*

* $p < .05$
** $p < .01$
*** $p < .005$
**** $p < .001$

Longer-term effects. Considerably fewer longer-term effects were noted than short-term effects (table 4). The self-report rating of depression on the POMS was significantly lower at baseline on day 5 than on day 1. Similarly, the behavior rating of anxiety was significantly lower at baseline on day 5 than on day 1. Surprisingly, despite this lower behavior rating of anxiety, saliva cortisol was significantly elevated on day 5 as compared with day 1.

Table 4. Means for Measures at Baseline, Days 1 and 5

	Day 1	Day 5	t value
Self-report			
State anxiety (STAIC)	32.9	30.5	N.S.
Depression (POMS)	16.9	10.1	3.21**
Behavior observation scale			
State	2.4	2.5	N.S.
Affect	1.9	1.8	N.S.
Activity	1.7	1.5	N.S.
Anxiety	1.8	1.4	2.93*
Fidgeting	1.6	1.5	N.S.
Vocalization	1.9	1.8	N.S.
Cooperation	2.8	2.6	N.S.
Activity level (Actometer)	6.7	5.3	N.S.
Pulse (BPM)	88.8	86.3	N.S.
Cortisol (ng/ml)	1.0	1.7	2.63*

* $p < .05$
** $p < .01$

Implications

These data are consistent with the literature on relaxation therapies suggesting decreases in anxiety and depression following treatment sessions (McGrady et al., 1981; Reynolds & Coats, 1986; Richter, 1984). Following the massage sessions, the patients' self-reported scores of anxiety and depression dropped significantly, their activity levels dropped, and they exhibited less anxious behavior. The consistency of the self-report and the behavior observation data support the use of this treatment for children and adolescents on psychiatric units.

Less impressive were the changes noted across the 5-day treatment period, suggesting that the longer-term effects were less significant than short-term effects. Decreased anxiety was manifested only by decreases in anxiety behavior ratings and not by self-report ratings. One possible interpretation is suggested by the cortisol data. Although cortisol decreased significantly on the first day of the study when comparisons were made between values taken before and after the massage session, no such decrease was noted from pre-session to post-session values on the fifth day. Moreover, although differences were not expected between cortisol levels on day 1 and day 5 because salivary cortisol is a phasic measure — that is, salivary cortisol levels do not typically change from day to day — baseline levels on day 5 were inflated as compared with day 1, suggesting that the subjects may have been more aroused in general on day 5. Day 5 was always a Friday, and Fridays are invariably high-anxiety days on child/adolescent psychiatric units, both for those patients who have earned weekend passes and are anticipating anxiety-producing interactions outside the hospital and for those who are "remaining alone" on the unit over the weekend. This phenomenon may have been working against the expected positive longer-term effects of the massage treatment and may have biased our results to date. Accordingly, we are rescheduling the massage therapy program so that baseline and follow-up assessments are both made midweek.

It is still not clear whether the specific treatment effect in our previous RT study (Platania et al., 1989) was related to massage, because we have not yet compared the massage treatment with other components. With an increase in sample size, the massage treatment will be compared with progressive muscle relaxation involving visual imagery and with a television-viewing control group. When we have a sufficiently large sample, we will also compare the effects on depressed patients versus those on adjustment disorder patients. Finally, the time-lapse videotapes will be analyzed for sleep-pattern changes, and the 24-hour urine samples for catecholamine changes. In the interim, the behavioral and self-report data themselves, along with subjective ratings made by clinical staff, suggest that the massage treatment may be effective for hospitalized child and adolescent psychiatric patients.

DISCUSSION

Most child and adult psychiatric units have a no-touch policy. Touching psychiatric patients has been so strongly tabooed that the Round Table participants were curious to know how the massage intervention had been received by both the subjects and the staff. Dr. Larson reported that the children and adolescents respond positively to the massage, although a few of the adjustment disorder children are very active and getting them to comply is more difficult. They all like being singled out for special attention, and there is a question as to whether the massage itself is having an additional effect. If TV-viewing control conditions can be considered special attention, the early RT study suggests that it is; in that study, in which the same subjects were studied in a TV-viewing condition and in the RT condition, no changes were found in the subjects in the TV condition, but changes were seen in the RT condition. The psychiatric and nursing staff welcomed the study, because they had seen the effectiveness of RT classes conducted on the unit.

Possible differences within the study population were raised. Comparisons among age groups have not yet been made, and Dr. Brazelton predicted that differences might well be seen between adolescents and preadolescents. Being massaged demands a kind of passivity that may be very hard for adolescents but not for preadolescents, he commented. Dr. Larson reported that no sex differences have been seen in the outcomes so far, although there tend to be more boys than girls in the adjustment disorder category. Dr. Older noted that contrary to his expectations he had seen teenage boys on a psychiatric ward responding well to massage.

One area where differences may well be found with a larger population is in the diagnostic groups. In the earlier study (Platania et al., 1989), just one difference was seen between the two diagnostic categories in the sample, depressed patients and adjustment disorder (or conduct disorder) patients. All the adjustment disorder subjects showed a sharp drop in cortisol levels, on the order of 50 percent, whereas among the depressed subjects, about a third showed a drop in cortisol, a third stayed the same, and a third showed a rise in cortisol level. Dr. Schanberg postulated that for the adjustment disorder group, being put on a psychiatric ward exacerbates their sense of isolation, and that these subjects have a need for touching, whereas the depressives have a biological problem. Dr. Brazelton concurred, noting that it would be a mistake to look for a single effect and that a rise in cortisol may in fact be evidence of an internal conflict that is not reflected in external behavior. Conduct disorder — now called adjustment disorder — is less a psychiatric diagnosis than a socioeconomic one, Dr. Older commented.

THERAPEUTIC TOUCH: RESEARCH ON THE HEALING RELATIONSHIP

Patricia Heidt, Ph.D., R.N.

Research to date on therapeutic touch (TT) has primarily used experimental methodology to focus on the effects of TT in such areas as state anxiety level (Heidt, 1981; Quinn, 1984) and pain (Keller & Bzdek, 1986; Meehan, 1985). The study reported here utilized a qualitative approach in an attempt to identify the inner experience — in both the person giving and the person receiving TT — that facilitates healing. Three major patterns of experience were found in both nurses and patients, in what is clearly a healing *interaction.*

Earlier Studies in Therapeutic Touch

Therapeutic touch is an intervention derived from the laying-on of hands. The potential for one person to help heal another through the use of hands has been found in cultures around the world since ancient times, but only recently has it been studied through scientific methodology. The groundbreaking research done with touch in nursing is attributed to Krieger (1974), who with her colleague Kunz coined the term *therapeutic touch* and studied its effects, first on hemoglobin levels in human subjects.

Influenced by Eastern philosophies, Krieger posited that the healthy person has an abundance of "life force," whereas the ill person has a deficit of this force. She conceptualized the relationshp between healer and healee as one in which

> the healthy individual is an open system of streaming energy in constant flux. . . . The ill person is one in whom this system has closed-in, so to speak upon himself. The role of the healer then would be concerned with helping the ill person to establish this vital flowing, open system; to restore, as it were, unimpeded communication with his environment (1974, p. 125).

The concept of a universal life force has been linked to what is known as field theory in Western scientific research. According to Jansch (1980), all living organisms share in a generalized life energy field. Rogers' (1970) conceptual framework in nursing views the universe as an open system in which the individual and the environment are energy fields that continually exchange energy with one another. As these living systems interact through the "rhythmical flow of energy waves," a repatterning takes place in the energy fields, toward a more complex and diverse order.

Applying this framework to the nurse-patient relationship in TT, one could characterize the nurse's field of energy as whole or well and the patient's as less open or less well. Through the field repatterning of TT, the patient's own self-healing mechanisms are stimulated, and the ability to regulate the many functions of the patient's living system is enhanced (Heidt, 1979).

In the first phase of TT, the person in the role of healer "centers," going within the self and finding the center of quiet and focused consciousness that Krieger likens to a meditative state. Next, the healer uses the hands to scan the energy level of the patient, sensing any differences from one part of the body to another. These may be sensed as differences in body temperature or felt as a sensation, such as tingling, on the surface of the hands. The assessment leads to a plan of treatment.

The treatment in TT consists of using the hands once again to redirect the areas of accumulated tension in the patient's body and/or to direct energy to the patient who has a deficit in field energy. Throughout the treatment process, the healer is always assessing the patient for a balance in the energy field. At a certain point, there is a sense that the field is flowing and balanced, and a decision to stop treatment is made (Krieger, 1979).

Krieger's research explored the relationship between TT and hemoglobin, a major physiological index. Professional registered nurses were the healers. In both the experimental and control groups, there were 32 patients and 16 nurses, each nurse working with 2 patients. The experimental group received a daily treatment of TT; the control group received routine hospital care. Pretest blood samples were drawn for both hemoglobin values and hematocrit ratios on all patients. TT was administered to the experimental group on two consecutive days by nurses trained by Krieger and/or Kunz. Post-test samples were drawn a minimum of four hours after the second TT treatment. All subjects were controlled for pretest hemoglobin values, circadian cycles, smoking, recent trauma, and history of recent change in vital signs. Patients were also screened for prior experiences in meditation and breathing exercises. The data supported the hypothesis that the mean hemoglobin values of patients treated by TT would be raised significantly following treatment by TT (Krieger, 1974).

A number of doctoral studies followed this research. One such study (Heidt, 1979) explored the effects of TT on the anxiety level of hospitalized cardiovascular patients. The sample was 90 volunteer male and female patients aged 29 to 65 and hospitalized on an inpatient cardiovascular unit. Each subject was administered the State-Trait Anxiety Inventory (STAI, Spielberger, Gorsuch, & Lushene, 1970) to measure the level of current anxiety. Subjects were matched and assigned to one of three groups, each of which received a five-minute period of intervention. The first group received intervention by TT, the second group intervention by casual touch (patients' pulse rate was taken in five body areas), and the third group a no-touch intervention (patients spent time talking with the nurse, without touch). After the intervention, the STAI was readministered. Patients receiving TT experienced a significant reduction in state anxiety, and this reduction was greater than that experienced by patients receiving casual touch or no-touch intervention (Heidt, 1979).

Quinn (1984) replicated this research, with two significant differences. First, the casual-touch group received an intervention that simulated TT in that the movements of TT were followed but the nurse did not "center." Second, the TT treatment group received an intervention in which the practitioner's hands were placed above the surface of the body rather than in direct contact with the body. The results of the study were almost identical with those of the original research.

Other doctoral research has studied the effects of TT in such areas as headache tension (Keller & Bzdek, 1986) and anxiety in elderly hospitalized patients (Parkes, 1985), in which positive effects were found, and postoperative surgical pain (Meehan, 1985), where beneficial effects have not yet been documented.

Research on TT lends support to the body of research and clinical practice showing the beneficial effects of interpersonal relationships on patient care. For a long time this aspect of care has been undervalued. With greater dependency on technological advances to aid recovery, the nurse-patient relationship and the effects of the "bedside manner" have been less appreciated. TT makes its unique contribution by offering a framework for understanding the potency of the human organism as a resource in healing (Heidt, 1981).

Qualitative Research in Therapeutic Touch

With the exception of Lionberger (1985), doctoral research in TT in the last decade has used experimental methodology. Current research is complementing these quantitative studies by using qualitative methods to understand the complexity of the healing relationship in TT (Heidt, 1989). In the present study, my goal was to begin to generate a body of theory concerning the nature of the healing interaction in TT by exploring the experiences of nurses and patients in giving and receiving TT.

To that end, I interviewed seven nurses and their patients and observed one treatment session of TT for each of the seven nurses and their patients. The nurses, all of whom had been taught by Krieger and/or Kunz, had practiced TT for 3 to 11 years (M = 9 years). The patients were not selected for any particular symptomatology. They had received from 10 to 100 TT treatments (M = 30).

The interviews and observations took place in the setting in which TT was usually administered. Interviews were based on broad questions, such as "Walk me through the treatment process of TT. What was your experience as you did this? What is it like to receive (or to give) a TT treatment? When TT works (or doesn't work), what is your experience?" Certain words and phrases in the respondents' answers were followed up with questions such as "You mentioned the word *energy*. What is your experience of that word?" Interview time for nurses was about 90 minutes, for patients 50 minutes. Each interview was preceded by an observation of a treatment session of TT, during which all body movements and all verbal and nonverbal communication between nurse and patient were recorded.

Grounded theory methodology (Glaser & Strauss, 1967) was used to collect and analyze these data. This process uses observations and interviews collected from the environments in which participants live. The constant comparative process analyzes new data with each previously collected piece of data, and through a continuous abstraction process the researcher is led toward the central theme as a pattern that links data and becomes the basis for theory generation. First-level coding consisted of noting all words and phrases that characterized the content of the interview and observational data. Second-level coding abstracted these data to a meaningful level. Eight categories emerged that expressed the experiences of nurses and patients giving and receiving TT: *quieting, affirming, intending, attuning, planning, unblocking, engaging,* and *enlivening*. In further analysis to find a core variable to link all eight categories of experiences, the experience of *opening* emerged as the basic social process. For nurses and patients in the study, TT was experienced as opening to the universal life energy. Openness was defined as the experience of (1) allowing oneself to focus intent on getting the universal life energy moving again, (2) assessing the quality of its flow, and (3) participating in a healing relationship that unblocks, engages, and enlivens its movement. Categories of experience were then grouped: quieting, affirming, and intending were grouped into *opening intent*, attuning and planning were grouped into *opening sensitivity*, and unblocking, engaging, and enlivening were grouped into *opening communication* (table 5).

Table 5. Therapeutic Touch: Opening the Flow of the Universal Life Energy.

Opening Intent	*Quieting*: Stilling the mind, emotions, and body to feel in harmony with the universal life energy *Affirming*: Recognizing the unity and wholeness of the universal life energy *Intending*: Desiring to get the universal life energy moving again
Opening Sensitivity	*Attuning*: Listening to the quality of the flow of the universal life energy *Planning*: Using the internal and external cues about the flow of the universal life energy to make a plan of treatment
Opening Communication	*Unblocking*: Clearing out the impediments and balancing the flow of the universal life energy *Engaging*: Directing and receiving the flow of the universal life energy *Enlivening*: Pulling in and balancing the flow of the universal life energy

The nurses' and patients' experiences of TT were very similar in a variety of ways. The data indicated that instead of having two separate categories of experiences, they had complementary experiences. Each category was therefore defined in a manner that included both nurses and patients. For example, all the nurses experienced wanting to help their patients, and all the patients wanted to be helped. Similarly, both nurses and patients described the experience of assessing the flow of energy. One nurse stated,

> I am trying to be aware of anything I feel differently in my hands. Like today, I was trying to move them slowly and smoothly down the field of the body, which is a few inches away from the body. When I feel they are not going down as smoothly, I know there is heaviness. I am searching for changes in the [energy] field.

A patient in describing her experiences said,

> I try to think of those places where the healer is assessing and do my own assessment. Like, I was thinking whether my teeth were hurting me and relaxing my jaw. And then she went here [pointing to chest] and I was aware of the tightness in my chest.

All the nurses expressed their experience of TT in terms of viewing themselves and their patients as "fields of energy." They spoke of qualities related to this energy: a healing force, a higher power, an organizing force, universal power, a greater mind. The images they used were the sun, God, an ocean of energy permeating the earth, light, and love.

All the patients but one experienced TT in terms of an energy. That one said that "it" was something leaving the body: "If you want to call it energy, for lack of a better word, okay. I don't pretend to know about that." Images used by patients for this energy were sunlight, God, a higher source, "the stuff we are all made of and that flows through everyone," the source of life, and flowing water.

A common term was sought to unite the nurses' and the patients' experiences. The original term, *life force*, was rejected by several participants; *universal life energy* was found acceptable to all participants.

Throughout the observations and interviews, it was clear that TT was not so much a healing act as a healing interaction. In their comments about their relationship to each other, the nurses and patients expressed an openness to the flow of the life energy between them. Patients said, for example, "I trust her a lot"; "He's a mentor to me"; and "We laugh and talk a lot together." Nurses in turn confirmed the necessity for building a sense of trust and sincerity into their relationship with the patient. They also spoke about the relationship with the patient as one in which they were a "channel" for the universal life energy; that is, they went within themselves and quietly focused on this life energy, with the intent to help their patients in this interaction, directing the energy where it was needed.

During the TT treatment sessions, in addition to using their hands to "unblock" areas of tension in the body physically, nurses also talked with their patients about issues of concern and communicated a friendly, open, and trustful attitude to them. Touch was not limited to the physical senses; touching therapeutically included giving and receiving information and the affective component of caring as well as the physical sense of touching.

Because early research used objective methodology to explore the nature of TT, it has not previously been possible to explore the nature of the nurse-patient relationship in TT. This aspect has been relegated to the status of placebo, as is customary in experimental methodology. One of the outcomes of this current research is that it may open a way to focus on the many interpersonal experiences that make up a healing relationship.

DISCUSSION

The participants were generally impressed with what they heard and saw as Dr. Heidt demonstrated therapeutic touch and reported on its effects. For some of them, however, various concepts and terminology of TT were stumbling blocks, especially the idea of a life energy or an electrical field surrounding the body. Dr. Gewirtz expressed the view that the behavioral sciences already have a range of concepts that can be used to explain the effects of TT and other situations in which people come to feel better when someone pays attention to them and shows concern. He speculated that the healing effects of TT might be understood more readily if behavior-science concepts shown to be useful in organizing very similar social processes were used for TT effects. Further, Dr. Gewirtz wondered what would have happened in the research with teenagers on the psychiatric ward (see Larson, this volume) if someone had watched television with the control group. Would the cortisol levels in that group have gone down, as they did in the treatment group?

Dr. Reite agreed, stating that the well-known placebo effect is still the most potent influence that physicians and other healers have at their disposal. So long as the person who is doing the therapy believes that it is going to help, the person who is being treated believes that the treatment is going to help, and some kind of therapeutic relationship is established, one will always be able to measure a statistically significant improvement. The mechanisms of the placebo effect are still not understood, he noted, and we should try to understand them better, but he does not see a need to invoke other forms of energy to explain it.

Dr. Schanberg cited studies that brought home the strength of the placebo effect. In one study of the effect of various analgesics on postoperative pain, the placebo relieved about 45 percent of the pain. Aspirin, codeine, and morphine relieved increasingly larger percentages of pain, respectively, but even with maximum doses of morphine the percentage was in the low 70s. Thus the difference between the best analgesic and the placebo was about 25 percent. Similarly, research in pharmacological treatment of depression has found a narrow therapeutic effect between the best recorded antidepressant and a placebo.

Part of the problem with terms such as "energy fields" that scientists have trouble with, Dr. Meaney offered, is a tendency to confuse explanation and description. Scientists tend to take literally, as explanations, ideas that are really being advanced as metaphorical descriptions. If researchers in TT and other areas can keep this distinction clear, they and those in the scientific community will have a better basis on which to communicate.

Dr. Heidt believes that the human being is a field of energy, and all living organisms in the universe are also fields of energy. Through their interaction with one another, change, growth, and healing take place. However, she added, that metaphor can be a strong element in itself. If you ask a nurse to think of herself as a nurse healer, immediately there is an intent to heal. And that intent is the key to TT. Something happens inside, and one wishes to help the other person. It sounds trivial, but it is an unbelievably complex phenomenon (see table 5).

Whether or not they accepted the concept of the energy field as a real entity or as a metaphor for a very potent communication set up between healer and healee, the conference participants welcomed the work that is being done in the study of TT, which is opening up new possibilities to them. What we want to do in the whole field of medicine is to humanize it, Dr. Brazelton noted.

EFFECT OF TOUCH ON HOSPITALIZED PATIENTS*

Jeffrey D. Fisher, Ph.D.,
and Sheryle J. Gallant, Ph.D.

Researchers have just begun to study touch with human adults, and the limited work to date suggests that the effects of touch with adults may be either positive or negative. Kleinke (1977), for example, reported that touch led to greater compliance with requests, and Fisher, Rytting, and Heslin (1976) observed that females who were touched experienced more positive affective and evaluative reactions than no-touch controls. On the other hand, Walker (1971) reported that communication by means of touch made subjects feel anxious and uncomfortable, and Henley (1973a) observed that touch may be perceived as exploitative and/or as highlighting the lower status of the recipient. It has also been shown that the same touch may be experienced positively by one sex and negatively by the other (Fisher, Rytting, & Heslin, 1976; Nguyen, Heslin, & Nguyen, 1975).

A review of past research with adult populations suggests that whether touch is experienced positively or negatively depends on the meaning and evaluation inferred by the recipient (Fisher, Rytting, & Heslin, 1976). Clearly, touching a person can mean many things, such as a desire for intimacy, sexual attraction, or dominance. Fisher, Rytting, and Heslin (1976) suggested that adults will experience a touch as positive to the extent that it (1) is appropriate to the situation, (2) does not impose a greater level of intimacy than the recipient desires, and (c) does not communicate a negative message (for example, is not perceived as condescending). These criteria have been supported in empirical work (for example, Hall, 1966; Henley, 1973a; Nguyen, Heslin, & Nguyen, 1975).

*Portions of this paper are adapted from "Multidimensional reaction to therapeutic touch in a hospital setting," by S. J. Whitcher & J. D. Fisher, 1979, *Journal of Personality and Social Psychology* 37(1): 87-96.

Predicting the Effects of Touch in a Hospital Context

In predicting the effects of touch in a setting characterized by dependency, such as a hospital, some important factors should be taken into account. In such a setting, touch can convey a mixture of positive (for example, caring) and negative (for example, power or dominance) elements. This interpretive ambiguity is exacerbated by the fact that in a physical sense, touches that express negative aspects of dependency such as inferiority and those that express positive aspects of caring and concern are quite similar (Henley, 1977; Heslin, 1976). Thus, competing rationales exist for predicting which of these two messages will be most salient in an interaction where a nurse touches a patient.

One prediction stems from research on gender differences in socialization. It is assumed that males are socialized to be more uncomfortable with dependency than females (Hoffman, 1972; Maccoby, 1966; Stein & Bailey, 1973). Because touches signaling dependency and those expressing caring may be physically similar, it is believed that socialization may importantly affect their interpretation. Thus, females may interpret nurse-patient touch as a primarily positive message of caring and warmth, which is situationally appropriate and of a reasonable level of intimacy (see Fisher, Rytting, & Heslin, 1976). On the other hand, males may react negatively because they interpret the nurse's touch as conveying a message of relative inferiority and dependency, which is neither situationally appropriate nor of a comfortable level of intimacy. In effect, it is suggested that touch in a dependency context is more sex role-appropriate for females than for males and should therefore lead to more positive female than male responses.

An opposing prediction centers on the special status that may be accorded to dependency that results from illness. Specifically, when one is a patient, being dependent may be socially acceptable for both sexes. In this interpretation, it would be expected that both males and females would interpret nurse-patient touch as an expression of caring that is situationally appropriate and of a reasonable level of intimacy. If this hypothesis were supported, males and females should have similar, positive reactions.

Method

The subjects were 48 patients (19 males, 29 females) who had entered a major university hospital for elective surgery. All had been assigned to primary nurses who had agreed to participate in the experiment. The patients were randomly assigned to experimental and control groups. Those in the control groups received normal hospital care and were exposed to customary professional/functional tactile contact with nurses. In the experimental conditions, nurses administered an additional touch manipulation during the preoperative teaching session.

The experimental manipulation took place shortly after admission. After closing the curtain surrounding the patient, the nurse touched the patient's hand for a few seconds while introducing herself and explaining that she was going to inform the patient about the surgery. Toward the end of the teaching session, the nurse gave the patient a booklet that further detailed the procedures for surgery. At that time, she put one hand on the patient's arm and maintained this touch for approximately one minute, while she and the patient examined the booklet. Patients in the control condition experienced the same preoperative teaching interaction, without the physical contact.

In both the experimental and control conditions, the nurse then extended her hand in a gesture suggesting contact and noted the patient's response as an unobtrusive measure of the subject's desire to reciprocate contact. She then left the room. Several hours later, the patient was approached by a male experimenter, who explained that the university was conducting a study of patient reactions to hospitalization and asked the patient to fill out a questionnaire, emphasizing that all responses were anonymous and confidential. The patient was asked to seal the completed form in an envelope, which was later collected by the experimenter.

The dependent measures used to assess the effects of touch represented a set of affective, evaluative, behavioral, and physiological indexes expected to discriminate between patients who react favorably and those who react unfavorably to the hospital experience. The *affective* measures consisted of three items assessing how anxious patients felt about undergoing surgery, how unpleasant it was for them to be in the hospital, and how worried they were about possible postoperative complications. *Evaluative* measures assessed satisfaction with preoperative instruction (there were two items asking patients how satisfied they were with information received and how satisfied they were with nursing care to that point) and attraction toward the nurse (there were three items asking how warm the patient perceived the nurse to be, how interested they felt the nurse was in their questions and feelings, and how friendly they felt toward the nurse).

The *behavioral* measures assessed two responses made by subjects during their hospital stay. On the assumption that touch might lead to differential reading of the booklet left by the nurse during the preoperative teaching, patients were asked how much of the booklet they had read. The second measure was the response of the patient to the nurse's proffered hand at the end of the teaching session, which was coded in terms of whether the patient grasped or touched the nurse's hand, reached toward her hand but did not touch it, looked at but did not touch her hand, or ignored her gesture.

Finally, the *physiological* measures included pulse and blood pressure data taken directly after surgery while the patient was in the recovery room and periodic vital signs measures (pulse, temperature, and blood pressure) collected during the first several days of hospitalization. Past research (for example, Martin, 1961) has shown that these indexes can be considered to discriminate between anxious and non-anxious patients.

Results

The findings on a variety of measures suggested that in a hospital setting, touch led to positive effects primarily for females. On affective dimensions, females who were touched reported less anxiety concerning surgery than control females, whereas males in the touch condition reported more anxiety than control males. Also, females were more anxious than males in control conditions, whereas males were more anxious than females in touch conditions.

On the behavioral measures, females in the touch condition read more of the booklet than controls; for males, the analysis was nonsignificant. Similarly, females in the touch condition more frequently reached out and touched the nurse's outstretched hand than controls, while for males touch did not make a significant difference.

Several physiological indexes also tended to show this pattern of positive reactions only for females. Recovery room vital signs indicated a significant Touch x Sex interaction for systolic blood pressure and a marginally significant Touch x Sex interaction for diastolic blood pressure. In both cases, at all five measurement intervals touch males tended to have higher readings than control males, whereas touch females tended to have lower readings than control females. Vital signs measurements taken in the room during the first few days of hospitalization revealed no main effects for touch, but data for both systolic and diastolic blood pressure indicated a trend toward significance for the effect of touch.

The overall pattern of results supports the sex difference hypothesis described above, which predicts that when dependency cues are pervasive, males and females will react differently to touch, because they have been socialized differently with respect to dependency. Other possibilities to explain the present data are also tenable, however. One centers on females' richer and more varied tactile history. Specifically, females are touched more often by a variety of others (mother, father, same/opposite-sex friends) than males (Jourard, 1966; Jourard & Rubin, 1968), and in other nonverbal modalities (for example, personal space) they display more permeable boundaries. Further, females probably have more exposure to tactile stimulation in medical contexts than males (for example, in yearly gynecological examinations and in giving birth). Hence, touch during preoperative teaching may have been reassuring for females but disruptive for males in part because males have less experience with touch in general and, more particularly, in medical contexts.

A second possibility stems from the fact that female patients interacted with a same-sex other, whereas males interacted with an opposite-sex other. Because there was no way to separate out the potentially confounding influence of sex of toucher from the effects of touch in the present setting, it is possible that being touched during preoperative teaching was a qualitatively different experience for males and females. For example, males could be more likely than females to interpret the present touch as sexual in nature. A study by Nguyen, Heslin, and Nguyen (1975), however, indicates that touches to the hand and/or shoulder, whether applied by a same-sex or opposite-sex other, are interpreted as nonsexual in nature. Nevertheless, it is not possible to rule out the above explanation solely on the basis of this study.

Implications

Past research tended to look at single rather than multiple responses to tactile stimulation. On the basis of this study, it appears that
touch may have consequences for affective state, behavior, and physiological reactions and that parallel effects may occur along all three
dimensions. Further, the data suggest that touch may have powerful
multidimensional effects over time, in addition to short-term effects.
It should be noted, however, that touch in the present study occurred
in a context where it was particularly salient and meaningful. While
touch in other situations of this type might be expected to have long-
term consequences, the effects of incidental tactile stimulation (see
Fisher, Rytting, & Heslin, 1976) or touch that is commonplace or role-
defined should be relatively short-term.

The present findings are in accord with Patterson's (1976) arousal
model of interpersonal intimacy, in which changes in intimacy produce arousal change, which may be a signal to evaluate and interpret
the environment. The change in arousal may be labeled as positive or
negative, depending on the context in which it occurs — for example,
socialization-related beliefs concerning touch and dependency. To
the extent that a positive label is engendered, it is assumed that
favorable reactions, such as positive affect or reciprocal intimacy, will
occur. For females in the present study, contextual factors may have
permitted a positive label for decreased arousal, which resulted in
favorable affective, physiological, and behavioral reactions. For males,
the context may have produced a negative labeling of increased
arousal, which resulted in unfavorable responses on these dimensions.
It is suggested that the fit of Patterson's model to the present data
indicates that it may be useful as an interpretive framework for past
research on touch and as a predictive framework for future work.

The results of this study may have practical implications for patient
care. Earlier research (for example, Johnson, Leventhal, & Dabbs,
1971) found that various conditions that facilitate low preoperative
anxiety improve patient recovery. In the present study, touch for
females resulted in lower anxiety and more positive behavior preop-
eratively, and these results were associated with more favorable
postoperative physiological responses. This finding suggests that touch
during preoperative teaching is a form of communication that may be
beneficial to the well-being of certain patients. Clearly, however, the
negative reactions of males in the present context prohibit any un-

qualified statements concerning the practical implications of the data. Before application will be possible, future research must assess the consequences of touch across a variety of medical settings and individual difference variables, in order to delineate more precisely the domain in which touch has beneficial effects.

DISCUSSION

Some participants questioned the fact that the nurses were all female, so that the males in the study, but not the females, were receiving opposite-sex touch. At the time of the study, there were very few males in nursing, and none was assigned to the floor where the study was done. Other studies have used both males and females to administer the touch, Dr. Fisher reported. In Fisher, Rytting, & Heslin (1976), for example, male and female librarians administered an unobtrusive touch to people checking books out of the library. The touch was found to have differential effects on males and females when they were subsequently asked to evaluate the library and its services, with women who were touched responding more favorably than controls and men who were touched responding in a more ambivalent fashion. Males in the experimental condition who had been touched by male librarians were particularly negative in their reactions, although very few of the subjects even recalled having been touched.

Dr. Brazelton suggested a somewhat different interpretation of the longer-term blood pressure effects for which the study indicated a trend toward significance for the effect of touch. In his experience, children undergoing cardiac surgery have better survival rates and recover more rapidly when the mother participates in preparing the child for surgery, making the preparation a more significant experience. He postulated that the touch effects in this study might be a combination of the females' greater receptivity to the preparation and the touch, which reinforced that receptivity.

Dr. Schanberg recalled reading a study done in a medical waiting room in which a large gender difference was found in patients' attitudes toward touching and interactiveness. Males were much more aggressive, angry, and unreceptive than females. In that state of unhappiness and loss of leadership, he commented, any sense of being patronized would be especially unacceptable and resented.

GENDER AND STATUS PATTERNS IN SOCIAL TOUCH: THE IMPACT OF SETTING AND AGE

Brenda Major, Ph.D.

Although touch has long been recognized as a significant means of nonverbal communication, relatively little research has been done to determine the correlates and meaning of touch. Early theories viewed touch primarily in terms of warmth and intimacy or sexual interest (see Jourard & Rubin, 1968). Henley (1973b, 1977), however, has argued that touch also conveys status and power. She proposed that the freedom to touch is a status privilege and therefore persons of higher status are more likely to touch persons of lower status than vice versa. She further proposed that male-to-female touch is more frequent than female-to-male touch and that these differences are due to the relative status of women and men in our society. Several observational studies failed to replicate Henley's findings, however, and the study reported here was designed to determine the degree to which the gender patterns she observed might be dependent on the setting in which the observations are made and the proportion of children in the sample. Both variables were found to be important.

Hypothesis 1: The Influence of Setting

Henley (1973b) tested her hypothesis in an observational study of 101 instances of intentional touch with the hand in a number of public settings. She found that men touched women more than women touched men, that touch from older persons to younger persons was more frequent than from younger to older, and that touch from persons of higher socioeconomic status (SES) to persons of lower SES was more frequent than from lower to higher. These data supported her hypothesis that touch is more frequent from high- to low-status persons than vice versa.

Henley's theoretical perspective has since become widely integrated into theories of nonverbal communication and sex roles. The observational studies that followed hers, however, failed to replicate the gender patterns she observed. For example, two studies of touch in airport settings (Greenbaum & Rosenfeld, 1980; Heslin & Boss, 1980) and one of touch in a bowling alley (Smith, Willis, & Gier, 1980) found no gender differences in touching behavior, leading some authors (for example, Stier & Hall, 1984) to question Henley's interpretation of touch as well as the assumption that touch varies as a function of gender.

Henley observed touch in a number of public, nonintimate settings such as shopping centers, a bank, and on campus. By contrast, the single settings in which subsequent researchers conducted their observations were ones in which touch may be less constrained and which may contain a high proportion of intimate or friendship dyads. Touch may reflect status with acquaintances and strangers but warmth with friends, lovers, and family members. Consequently, the current study hypothesized that sex differences in touch in accord with those observed by Henley might be observed in public, nonintimate settings, whereas sex differences might not be observed in greeting/leaving settings or recreational settings where a higher proportion of close or intimate dyads might be expected. Specifically, it was predicted that in public, nonintimate settings male-to-female touch would be more frequent than female-to-male touch, males would be more likely than females to be the initiators of touch, females would be more likely to be the recipients of touch than males, and cross-sex touch would be more frequent than same-sex touch. It was also predicted that these differences would not be observed in greeting/leaving or recreational settings.

Hypothesis 2: Dyads Containing a Child

A second hypothesis of this study is that sex differences in touching behavior may be affected by the proportion of children included in the sample. Studies of touch among children have failed to provide support for the touch patterns Henley observed (see Willis & Hofmann,

1975; Willis & Reeves, 1976; Willis, Reeves, & Buchanan, 1976). There are a number of reasons why touch between adults and children or from one child to another may convey a different message or serve a different purpose than touch between adults. There may be a higher proportion of family members included in dyads in which one member is a child. Females may be more likely to be the initiators of touch with children than males, because in our society child-rearing is more apt to be done by women. To the extent that status differences in touch may be a learned behavior, it might be expected that touch between children would not reflect the same gender differences observed in touch interactions involving adults. Furthermore, children might be expected not to have acquired adult reservations concerning same-sex touch; in fact, touch between same-sex playmates may be more frequent than touch between children of opposite sexes. The current study hypothesized that status and sex differences in touch might vary according to whether or not children were included in the sample. Specifically, it was predicted that when children were involved in touch, females would be significantly more likely than males to be the initiators of touch and that same-sex touch would be more frequent than cross-sex touch.

Method

The procedure was identical to that used by Henley. In eight different places in two cities, raters (4 male and 3 female, all blind to the hypotheses) recorded the sex, age, race, and approximate SES of initiators and recipients of 799 instances of intentional touch. Raters coded only those instances in which they observed the initiation of touch.

Result

The overall touch patterns were consistent with Henley's results. Male-to-female touch was significantly more frequent than female-to-male touch, females were significantly more likely to be the recipients of touch than were males, and males were somewhat more likely to be the initiators of touch than were females (table 6).

Table 6. Frequency of Touch by Sex of Initiator and Sex of Recipient (All Settings)

Sex of Initiator	Sex of Recipient	Entire Sample	Touches Involving Adults Only	Touches Involving Children
Male	Male	131	104	27
Male	Female	291	274	17
Female	Male	210	186	24
Female	Female	167	113	54
	Total N	799	677	122

Differences were found, however, when instances were categorized into three general types of settings: *public/nonintimate* (shopping malls and stores, outdoor downtown business districts, and campus), *greeting/leaving* (airports and bus stations), and *recreational* (outdoor parks and beaches, an art gallery, and a bar). The sample was also divided into touch involving adults only, in which the estimated age of both participants was at least 15 years, and touch involving children, in which at least one of the participants was estimated to be 14 years old or younger (table 6). Analyses of adult-only touch patterns were conducted separately for each of the three general settings. Because the number of touch instances involving children within each setting was too small for reliable analysis, analyses of touch involving children are presented collapsed across setting.

The hypothesis that sex differences in touching behavior vary according to the setting in which touch is observed was strongly supported in this study. As predicted, among adults in public/nonintimate settings, male-to-female touch was significantly more frequent than female-to-male touch. Males were significantly more likely to be the initiators of touch than were females, and females were significantly more likely to be the recipients of touch than were males. Opposite-sex touch was significantly more frequent than same-sex touch, and female-to-female touch was significantly more frequent than male-to-male touch.

By contrast, in greeting/leaving settings there were no significant differences in adult touch patterns as a function of sex. Male-to-female touch was not significantly more frequent than female-to-male touch, males were not significantly more likely to be the initiators of touch, and females were not significantly more likely to be the recipients of touch. Opposite-sex touch tended to be somewhat more frequent than same-sex touch, but female-to-female touch and male-to-male touch were equal.

Among adults in recreational settings, some sex differences did emerge, although the pattern was not as strong as that found in the public/nonintimate settings. Male-to-female touch was significantly more frequent than female-to-male touch. Males were significantly more likely to be the initiators of touch than were females, but females were not significantly more likely to be the recipients of touch. Opposite-sex touch tended to be more frequent than same-sex touch, and male-to-male touch tended to be more frequent than female-to-female touch.

In touch involving children, females were found to be significantly more likely to be the initiators of touch than were males and somewhat more likely to be the recipients of touch. Same-sex touch was significantly more frequent than opposite-sex touch, and female-to-female touch was significantly more frequent than male-to-male touch.

Of the two other status variables included in the study — SES and age — SES was found to be very difficult to determine, and the number of instances in which estimates of very high or very low SES were made were too few for reliable analysis. Age differences of at least five years between dyad members, however, did prove significant. For the entire sample across all three general settings, touch from older persons to younger persons was significantly more frequent than touch from younger to older. In the portion of the sample involving adults only, older-to-younger touch was also significantly more frequent than younger-to-older.

Conclusion

The results of the present study generally confirm Henley's hypotheses concerning sex and age differences in touch patterns. They further indicate, however, that the sex differences predicted by Henley are context-specific and apply only for adults. The data suggest that touch conveys several messages and cannot simply be seen as conveying only warmth or only status. This proposal is consistent with recent research on observers' perceptions of the meaning of nonreciprocal touch (Major & Heslin, 1982). Furthermore, this study resolves past inconsistencies regarding gender differences in touch by clarifying the critical nature of both the situation in which touch is observed and the ages of the participants involved.

DISCUSSION

Some of the participants found the observational data contrary to personal experience and debated what further refinement of the categories might reveal. For example, how does the gender effect interact with status in the case of high-power women? Dr. Major would anticipate the gender effect to be stronger in situations that provide weak or ambiguous cues to appropriate behavior; in a strong situation, where the rules of appropriate behavior are clear, the gender effect might be masked or attenuated. A woman boss might feel more comfortable touching a lower-status man, but controlling for status, one might still find that high-power women are less likely to touch men than high-power men are to touch women. Men may also be less likely to touch high-power women than to touch low-power women. Here the situational context may be a factor; touching behavior toward a professional woman may vary according to whether or not she is in her professional role.

Differences that were observed between adult-only interactions and interactions involving children raised the question of when children become socialized to the rules of sex differences in behavior. The study did not break down the instances of touch by age of the child. Several participants set the age of 12 or 13 as the turning point in behavioral differences, and if children are learning differences from the very beginning, divergences might be expected to be well established by this age. Some developmental theorists, however, suggest that greater sex differences are seen at the ages of 10, 11, and 12 than among adults.

Cultural differences were also introduced as an important factor in touching behavior. In Western culture, for example, there are taboos about males touching males. Ethnicity did not appear to enter into the results of this research, however, which was undertaken in two cities very different in their ethnic populations; it remains to be examined in future studies.

EPILOGUE:
TOUCH IN ALL AGES

Jules Older, Ph.D.

Let me tell you three stories.

On a cold, overcast day in the mountains of Utah, a Maryland neurosurgeon gazed apprehensively down a ski trail he was afraid was too tough for him to handle. He was right. He skied the first thirty yards, then took a tumble that hurled him head over heels into the deep snow. The surgeon was dazed when he finally came to a stop a long way down from where his fall had begun. As he regained his senses, he was certain of only one thing — that his neck was broken.

He never mentioned the break to the skier who raced to get help, nor to the ski patrollers who secured him to the sled, nor to the nurse in the first-aid station, where he lay perfectly still on a narrow bed. But as a neurosurgeon, he knew all too well the implications of a broken neck for his career and for his life as a man. The feeling of panic that started at that first moment of realization now swelled like a balloon expanding throughout his whole person.

The nurse was busy, but one glance at her silent patient stopped her in her tracks. She turned around, sat beside him on the bed, and silently took his hand in hers.

"As *soon* as she took my hand, I felt the panic lift. I'd never seen her before and still hadn't spoken to her, but the effect she had on me was almost magic. From complete panic to just about total calm in a few seconds. And all from the touch of a hand."

"What happened next?"

"When I got back to work I completely reorganized my approach to patients. I'm from a very un-touchy family, and I'd never been your warm, touching doctor — not many neurosurgeons are. But from that time on I've made it a point to touch most of my patients. I'd seen for myself what it could do. And it's had a tremendous effect on my relationship with them."

"What about your broken neck?"

"Strained muscle was more like it. Never diagnose yourself." (Older, 1982, p. 182)

* * *

If you have to have a motorcycle accident in Dunedin, the southern-most major city in New Zealand, the place to have it is at the intersection of Frederick and Great King Streets. On one corner sits the Wellcome Institute and the medical school. On the next is Dunedin Public Hospital. The third corner is filled with house-surgeon quarters. And if you've injured your teeth, you can get help from the institution on the fourth corner, the country's only dental school.

So the young motorcyclist who crashed his Yamaha at that intersection was, if not skilled enough to avoid an accident, lucky enough to have it in the right place. He was lying on the sidewalk in obvious pain and distress while legions of white-coated health-providers worked on his leg. There were ambulance drivers, house surgeons, medical consultants, and researchers who hadn't been out of the laboratory for years. They were climbing over one another in an attempt to get at that leg.

But there was no shortage of room at the motorcyclist's head. One lone young medical student cradled his head in her lap. She whispered soothing things in his ear while she stroked his cheeks lightly with the backs of her fingertips.

Perhaps she chose that position because she was one of the few women at the scene. But it's just as likely that she was the one person amongst that large and highly specialized crowd of health providers who had not yet been trained *out of* the skilled and comforting use of the hands for something other than pulse-taking, palpation, and bone-setting.

* * *

Third tale. Not long ago I served as a line judge at a high school track-and-field day. In the girls' 400-meter race, one of the competitors collapsed as she crossed the finish line. Her body was heaving; she couldn't find air. She was having an asthmatic attack, and I was the first to reach her. I heard another runner shout, "She forgot her inhaler! She's got asthma!"

Then everybody started shouting. Why is it that at accidents and emergencies, bystanders feel they must shout advice at whoever is closest to the victim? Voices were hollering, "Lie her down! Give her room! Get an ambulance!" and all the other things that people invariably holler at such times. I knelt beside her and placed my hand on her heaving back. Bringing my mouth close to her ear, I said in a quiet, steady voice, "Okay, you're all right. Now just breathe with me. When I breathe in, you do it with me." With that, I visibly inhaled, then exhaled, inhaled, then exhaled as she watched the rise and fall of my chest through frightened eyes.

It didn't work. We were too far out of synch for her to slow down to my breathing rate. I tried again, this time altering each breath only a little, slowly bringing her uncontrolled wheezing down to a regular pattern of inhale, exhale, inhale, exhale. Throughout the procedure I stayed close to her, rubbing big circles on her back. Gradually, her wheezing synchronized with my breathing. In less than five minutes, she was breathing normally and walked away from the track unassisted.

* * *

What these three examples have in common is the use of touch as an agent of healing. They show how this simple, most mammalian response can cut through panic, reduce shock, and repel an asthma attack. Touch can also build a bond of trust between doctor and patient, can release repressed material in psychotherapy, reduce the need for pain medication, ease a cramp, soothe a muscle. . . the list goes on and on. Yet few physicians are trained in touch.

I recently surveyed virtually every medical school in the English-speaking world and discovered that only 12 of 169 gave any training whatsoever in touch beyond that needed for pulse-taking, palpation, and the like. With the exception of the University of Otago (located at the corner of Frederick and Great King Streets in Dunedin, New Zealand), no school allotted more than two hours in the entire curriculum to touch as a healing agent. If the subject is thought of at all, most schools seem to expect that young doctors will "pick it up" in a way that they would never expect them — or *allow* them — to "pick up" heart sounds identification, x-ray reading, or knowledge of antibiotics.

I believe that our doctors will be better healers when they are more skilled at, and more comfortable with, touch. And I believe that that day will come only when medical schools teach touch alongside of (No, not instead of) other clinical skills. Leaving it to chance is not good enough.

This paucity of touch instruction is all the more surprising given the history of touch as an agent of healing. For no matter when in history you start or where in the world you look, whenever humans are sick, afraid, or in pain, touch is there. And no matter how arcane, bizarre, or technocratic the healing ritual, just below the surface explanation touch is at the heart of the practice. From chiropractic to Christian healing, rolfing to reflexology, touch is part of healing. From the mud spas of Europe to the curanderos of Cuba, from the rituals of the Navaho to the ritual of the annual check-up, touch is there.

Going back in history, you'll find the same story. The oldest known medical document of Egypt, the Papyrus Ebers, prescribed massage for hysteria. The earliest medical text from India, the *Ayur-Veda*, listed massage along with diet and exercise as the major health restorers. Chinese physicians of the T'ang dynasty elevated massage to one of the four officially recognized medical techniques some 5,000 years ago. The others were acupuncture, internal medicine, and exorcism.

On the subject of exorcism, physical contact has been part of that ancient rite at least since the time of Jesus, who also used touch for anointing and, of course, for the laying on of hands. Go into any charismatic church today and you will see that the force is still with us.

But whatever our healing roots, it is medicine to which most of us turn when we're sick. Here are some examples of touch at work in medicine of different forms for patients of different ages:

1. *Neonatology.* The most common minor disorder of infancy is cradle cap. Fortunately, it responds quickly to effective topical creams that are widely available. Why, then, would an eminent physician prescribe a relatively ineffective cream for treating the condition?

The answer is that the ineffective cream may help treat a much more difficult disorder, lack of attachment between parent and child. One way to build and strengthen a bond of attachment is to encourage regular, positive physical contact. Thus, when Professor H. Musaph of the University of Amsterdam is confronted with a case of cradle cap in an infant whose mother shows signs of difficulty in expressing affection, he reverses the usual treatment logic:

> We usually prescribe generously dosed topical therapy in children with cradle cap. However, if we feel that the baby is suffering from tactile neglect by the mother, we recommend that a less effective cream be rubbed into its skin five or six times first. The result is that its skin is stroked much more often, and this has a beneficial effect not only on the skin disorder but also on the child's general well-being. (Musaph, 1978, p. 11)

2. *General practice.* A farmer in his mid-30s makes an appointment for a check-up with his G.P. Tough, independent, and healthy, he has probably never sought a medical check-up in his life. The practitioner notes this and asks him in a number of ways if anything is wrong. Every question is answered, "No, things are fine."

Finally running out of questions, the doctor gives the apparently healthy farmer a physical examination. When it is complete, he sits down with him and says, "You appear to be in good health. I can find nothing wrong with you."

At this point the farmer's eyes tear up, and for the first time he talks about how worried he is about the state of his farm. It's on the verge of bankruptcy, and he has spent sleepless nights ruminating about it. He feels awful.

Why didn't the farmer simply tell his doctor this at the beginning? The G.P. thinks that what allowed the information to come out was the skin-to-skin contact of the physical examination:

> I felt clearly that I had been able to demonstrate to him, probably through touching him, that he could trust me and that he could now talk about it. If you examine people — and that means touching them — they'll often open out and tell you things that they quite clearly wouldn't have told you beforehand.
>
> Unfortunately, it's a lesson in scientific versus magic medicine. Scientifically, in half the people who come to see you there's really no need to examine them at all, or at least no need to touch them. By looking down their throats and asking questions you can be very clear of the diagnosis without touching people.
>
> But it's often important to do what might be called a therapeutic examination, or, more accurately, a trust-forming or relationship-cementing examination. This does involve touch. It tells your patient three things: (a) that you're a proper doctor, (b) that you can be trusted, and (c) that you're not scared to have this sort of contact with people. (Older, 1982, pp. 164-65)

3. *Surgery.* With the possible exception of pathology, surgery seems the least likely branch of medicine to involve touch. After all, most major surgery is done under general anesthetic, when touch is of little apparent consequence. But the patient is not anesthetized until just before surgery, and there is considerable evidence that patients' attitudes about an impending operation affect their speed of recovery from it.

A few years ago I had the pleasure of following Dr. Alan Clark, Professor of Surgery at the University of Otago, for a week as he made his morning rounds. I observed that in both pre- and postoperative visits he always sat close to his patients and invariably found one reason or another to lay hands on them. In one of his preoperative visits, he sat on the bed of a woman in her late 40s, slapped his large hand on her thigh, and said, "Well, Mavis, are you ready for surgery?"

She slapped her hand on *his* thigh and answered, "More to the point, Doctor — are you?"

The comfort these two — surgeon and patient — felt with one another was both made obvious and strengthened by reciprocal touch. It is hard to imagine either surgeon or patient in a better frame of mind and body for major surgery. Such use of touch should be at least as valuable to anesthetists as to surgeons.

4. *Radiology.* Like surgery, radiology seems an unlikely discipline to employ touch. I used to think so myself, but a letter from an Otago colleague changed my mind:

> Having a C.T. Scan affords many opportunities for being touched by the staff. This includes radiographers, nurses, and doctors. We have had a small discussion this morning and we are all very much aware that we touch our patients a great deal while getting them on and off the platform, adjusting their position and administering contrast material. While there are obviously many aspects of high technology diagnostic equipment which can be debated, I feel in the local setting that the C.T. Scanner is actually increasing the opportunity for our patients being touched and therefore hopefully contributing to healing in this way. (Personal communication, 1984)

5. *Psychiatry.* This example is from my own experience as a clinical psychologist, but it could just as easily have come from the case notes of a psychiatrist. It involves a floridly psychotic patient and demonstrates how physical contact can be used as a ground control to bring a high flyer down to earth.

I interviewed the young woman on a psychiatric ward. Although the interview took place in New Zealand, the patient informed me that we were actually in India, where she had just arrived from outer space. And she was clearly heading back into orbit as we talked.

I asked her permission to take her hand, and, from somewhere in the galaxy, she gave it. As I held her hand in mine, the effect was rapid and easily observed. Within three or four minutes she was no longer in Bengal or the Milky Way but back in the room with me. After a few minutes of sane conversation I released her hand, and very slowly her delusional speech returned. It was my physical contact with her that was literally keeping her in touch with the world.

6. *Gerontology.* Just as touch can bring the psychotic patient down to earth, so can it bring elderly, senile patients at least temporarily back to reality. In fact, physical contact may be one of the few means available for getting and holding their attention. Resting a hand on the arm, holding hands, combing hair, and massage are all effective ways of keeping a senescent mind attending to the present moment. Touch also helps establish an easy rapport with elderly patients and, if handled with sensitivity, will be accepted with gratitude.

7. *Pathology.* For the sort of pathologist who does nothing but autopsies, I concede the point — touch skills are going to be of no use. But for the pathologist who deals with relatives of accident victims, wives of murdered men, and parents of young children who have just died from unknown causes, being skilled in touch will be of great use and of great comfort to the people they see.

The distinguished scientist-physician Lewis Thomas (1983) summed up the need for touch in medicine as follows:

> There, I think, is the oldest and most effective act of doctors, the touching. Some people don't like being handled by others, but not, or almost never, sick people. They need being touched, and part of the dismay in being very sick is the lack of close human contact. Ordinary people, even close friends, even family members, tend to stay away from the very sick, touching them as infrequently as possible for fear of interfering, or catching the illness, or just for fear of bad luck. The doctor's oldest skill in trade was to place his hands on the patients.

> Over the centuries, the skill became more specialized and refined, the hands learned other things to do beyond mere contact. They probed to feel the pulse at the wrist, the tip of the spleen, or the edge of the liver, thumped to elicit resonant or dull sounds over the lungs, spread ointments over the skin, nicked veins for bleeding, but the same time touched, caressed, and at the end held on to the patient's fingers. (p. 56)

APPENDIX: RESEARCH ISSUES
AND DIRECTIONS

By the close of the second day of the Round Table, there was general agreement among the participants that to issue guidelines with respect to touch would be premature. What the conference had brought forth was not clear-cut answers but a heightened sense of the complexity of touch and of interrelationships with other systems. Much remains to be learned before recommendations regarding the clinical implementation of touch can be made with confidence. The final morning, therefore, was devoted to a discussion of the research and clinical issues pertaining to touch that remain to be explored. What follows is a brief summary of the ideas that emerged.

Ironically, touch is one of the first systems to develop in the human and in lower organisms yet the last sensory system to be given attention. There are institutes for the study of all the other senses but none for touch, and too few researchers are working on touch. Part of the problem may be that people think of touch as an amorphous, nonspecific system, whereas in fact it is very specific and definable. Another problem is that touch is virtually impossible to eliminate empirically without destroying the normal functioning of the organism; with every other sensory system, it is possible to study the ways the system contributes to the organism by means of experiments in which that sensory input is eliminated. Nor do cases occur in nature, comparable to those who have been blind or deaf from birth, that can be studied. Still, it is possible to design research that focuses on quantifiable effects while controlling for other things. Most research, however, has not separated the influence of touch from the impact of relationship changes. Regarding such studies, there was a divergence of opinion. Some participants expressed the belief that breaking down the touch system into its components — for example, mapping specific stimulatory patterns and skin receptors — is essential to our learning. Others, however, considered any causal stimulus/response to be too simple an empirical model for the complexity of the touch system and insisted upon a systems approach.

It is already well established that touch is an extraordinarily important sensory modality for development, both physiological development and social development. What is needed now is to go back to specific paradigms and look at how the information is transmitted by touch and what specific effect it has. We need to know more about the functions and meanings of different kinds of touch and how these meanings are transmitted from parent to child.

Animal models as well as human models will be important in finding answers to the many questions about touch, and much can be gained by greater interaction between the two types of research. Animal studies can be used to understand mechanisms that cannot be explored in humans. Those working with humans can identify questions that need answers. As in the study of massage with adolescent psychiatric patients (Larson, this volume), a neurochemist can identify a physiological measure to be assessed along with behavioral effects; in that study the result was the discovery of a difference that would have been missed if the mechanism had not been examined at the more basic level. A productive and continuing interaction and discussion between those working with humans and those working with animals can contribute to each other's work and result in the design of studies that take our understanding further faster.

The practical problems of engaging in this kind of multidisciplinary collaboration, however, are formidable. Funding for such collaborative efforts is very difficult to obtain. People would like to be working together more, but they are constrained by limited time and space and by the demands of their short-term grants. An institute for touch could be a tremendous impetus to research in this area, demonstrating a recognition of the importance of touch, fostering careers in touch research, and providing a valuable resource for those doing behavioral research.

Other kinds of methodological models are also making important contributions to research in touch. Cross-cultural and evolutionary models can reveal the operation and interaction of different conditions that lead to a wider range of outcomes. In fact, many of the practices currently under study—infant massage, the use of doulas, holding and carrying—have come from technologically simple societies. Adopting a practice from such a culture, however, raises some basic questions about the appropriateness of the effects to our society. For example, reducing infants' crying (see Barr, this volume) would intuitively appear to be a desirable goal, yet it is possible that allowing infants to get into an extremely distressed state in which they must self-console and self-calm may be preparing them for coping with stress in our society.

We are in fact extremely selective in what we choose to adopt from these technologically simple societies. Our cultural values are important in determining our touch practices, and many of the practices that we value today are completely unknown in such cultures. For example, the father's presence at delivery is totally abiologic; there are almost no species where males are present at delivery, and it is unknown in technologically simple societies, but most people would agree that it has powerful benefits. In such areas research will tend to be weighed against cultural values.

In studies of the clinical uses of touch, variability cannot be understood in terms of the touch alone; it is essential to define the setting in which touch occurs, the relationship within which it occurs, the intentional messages that are conveyed, the appropriateness of the intentionality, and in the case of touch with infants, the state of the infant. If all the contextual ingredients are defined, we can learn from failures to replicate the study. Research often does not define how much of a relationship is made with patients, yet this is an important variable; effects are obtained in control groups just by making enough of a relationship with patients to keep them coming back for follow-up visits.

Of the clinical populations for whom touch is critical, the areas of greatest concern are infants and infant-parent relationships. Touch affects the infant in a number of ways, as an organizer of state and as an enhancer of indirect effects to bring out direct messages, such as "Here I am," "let's play," and "I love you." In the case of the infant, the indirect effects are probably critical, transmitting signals of the baby's state and the intentionality of the adult that lead us to understand what is appropriate and inappropriate within the affective intersubjective states. In the way these messages are transmitted by touch, the variations from culture to culture are more apparent than actual. The goal of every culture and every species is to use dependency and attachment as a way of achieving detachment and independence. Within that concept, we must consider individual differences in the baby and in the parent-infant interaction and expectations.

The parent needs to be considered as part of a culture, within a system, and alone. In our culture we have lost the value of touch and the communication it brings, and parents come to parenting with expectations from their own past, which may not have included optimal communication. Touch can become a powerful way of learning their role and learning about the infant as a system. And the communication of messages and expectations via touch is so powerful that it is an area that warrants immediate study.

In addition to infants and parents, there are several populations among whom touch offers promise for therapeutic benefits. The elderly often experience loss of touch when one partner dies, and the death of a spouse is known to have effects on the immune system and health and survival. For the dying, touch is often the last sense to survive; massage could be an excellent medium for maintaining the bond between the person dying and the one who is to survive. Many acquired immune deficiency syndrome (AIDS) patients are isolated, without strong support systems, and touch could play an important role in their treatment. Child abusers are examples of touch gone wrong; they may need it most. Touch may prove of use in substance withdrawal; a high percentage of cocaine abusers are said to have been physically and/or sexually abused. Touch will be critical with addictive babies; as they withdraw, we need to know how to use containment and holding and tactile stimulation to bring them back into contact with their environments.

Treatment practice does not always require scientific justification; in certain cases there may be good reasons to act without waiting for the research. At the same time, it is important to keep in mind the difference between efficacy studies and effectiveness studies. An efficacy study shows that in a best-of-all-possible-worlds situation, an effect is obtained. An effectiveness study moves that operation into a real-life situation, with all the uncontrollable factors that did not exist in the first situation, and determines whether the effect is still there. Both kinds of study need to be done for questions of therapeutic intervention to ensure that in the real world — with, for example, less skilled people doing the intervention — the interventions do not do more harm than good.

Yet even in efficacy studies, the touch of one experimenter may produce a negative outcome where all other touchers (nurses participating in the experiment) obtain a positive effect. Training in touch is clearly a critical area in need of study.

Touch in all its many forms carries an enormous contextual opportunity to hold and contain the lonely human family, which right now needs to be given some feeling that we do have cultural values that are worthwhile, true, and fair. Touch is extremely complex, and determining what it does to the human system is a major challenge. We must first break it down to understand the systems it is affecting, but then we must put it back together again to get at the true complexity.

REFERENCES

Abu-Osba, Y., Brouillette, R., Wilson, S., & Thach, B. 1982. Breathing patterns and transcutaneous oxygen tension during motor activity in preterm infants. *American Review of Respiratory Disease* 125(4):382-387.

Ader, R., & Grota, L. 1969. Effects of early experience on adrenocortical reactivity. *Physiology and Behavior* 4:303-305.

Agarwal, K.N., & Agarwal, D.K. 1981. Infant feeding in India. *Indian Journal of Pediatrics* 49:285.

Als, H., Lawhon, G., Brown, E., Gibes, R., Duffy, F., McAnulty, G., & Blickman, J. 1986. Individualized behavioral and environmental care for the very low birth weight preterm infant at high risk for bronchopulmonary dysplasia: Neonatal intensive care unit and developmental outcome. *Pediatrics* 78(6):1123-1132.

Ambrose, A. (Ed.). 1969. *Stimulation in early infancy.* New York: Academic Press.

Anisfeld, E., & Lipper, E. 1983. Early contact, social support and mother-infant bonding. *Pediatrics* 72:79-83.

Antoni, F. 1986. Hypothalamic control of ACTH secretion: Advances since the discovery of 41-residue corticotropin-releasing factor. *Endocrine Reviews* 7:351-370.

Bailey, R.C., & Peacock, N.R. In press. The Efe pygmies of northeast Zaire: Subsistence strategies in the Ituri Forest. In I. de Garine & G.A. Harrison (Eds.), *Uncertainty in food supply.* London: Oxford University Press.

Barber, T. 1976. *Pitfalls in human research.* New York: Pergamon.

Barnard, K. 1973. The effect of stimulation on the sleep behavior of the premature infant. *Communicating Nursing Research* 6:12-40.

Barnard, K., & Bee, H. 1983. The impact of temporally patterned stimulation on the development of preterm infants. *Child Development* 54:1156-1167.

Barnett, C., Leiderman, P., Grobstein, R., & Klaus, M. 1970. Neonatal separation: The maternal side of interactional deprivation. *Pediatrics* 45:197-205.

Barr, R. In press. Recasting a clinical enigma: The case of infant crying problems (or colic). In P. Zelazo & R. Barr (Eds.), *Challenges to developmental paradigms: Implications for theory, assessment, and treatment.* Hillsdale, N.J.: Erlbaum.

Barr, R., Bakeman, R., Konner, M., & Adamson, L. 1987. Crying in !Kung infants: Distress signals in a responsive context. *American Journal of Diseases of Children* 141:386.

Barr, R., Hunziker, U., McMullan, S., Speiss, H., Leduc, D., Yaremko, J., Barfield, R., Francoeur, T., & Rossy, P. 1989. Carrying as colic "therapy": A randomized controlled trial. *American Journal of Diseases of Children* 143:435.

Barr, R., Konner, M., Bakeman, R., & Adamson, L. 1987. Crying in !Kung infants: A test of the cultural specificity hypothesis. *Pediatric Research* 21:178A.

Bayley, N. 1969. *Manual for the Bayley scales of infant development.* New York: Psychological Corp.

Beaumont, K., & Fanestil, D.D. 1983. Characterization of rat brain aldosterone receptors reveals high affinity for corticosterone. *Endocrinology* 113:2043-2051.

Beisel, W., Edelman, R., Nauss, K., & Suskind, R. 1981. Single nutrient effects on immunologic functions. *Journal of the American Medical Association* 245:53-58.

Bell, S., & Ainsworth, D. 1972. Infant crying and maternal responsiveness. *Child Development* 43:1171-1190.

Blackburn, S., & Barnard, K. 1985. Analysis of caregiving events relating to preterm infants in the special care unit. In A. Gottfried & J. Gaiter (Eds.), *Infant stress under intensive care.* Baltimore: University Park Press.

Blaney, P. 1981. The effectiveness of cognitive and behavior therapies. In L. Rehm (Ed.), *Behavior therapy for depression: Present status and future directions.* New York: Academic Press.

Blurton Jones, N. 1972. Comparative aspects of mother-infant contact. In N. Blurton Jones (Ed.), *Ethological studies of child behavior.* Cambridge, England: Cambridge University Press.

Boccia, M., Laudenslager, M., & Reite, M. 1988. Food distribution, dominance, and aggressive behaviors in bonnet macaques. *American Journal of Primatology* 16:123-130.

Boccia, M., Laudenslager, M., & Reite, M., unpublished. Food dispersal, aggression, and response to maternal separation in bonnet macaque infants.

Boccia, M., Reite, M., & Laudenslager, M. 1989. On the physiology of grooming in a pigtail macaque. *Physiology and Behavior* 45:667-670.

Box, G., & Jenkins, G. 1968. *Time series analysis: Forecasting and control.* San Francisco: Holden Day.

Brackbill, Y. 1973. Continuous stimulation reduces arousal level: Stability of the effects over time. *Child Development* 44:43-45.

Brazelton, T.B. 1962. Crying in infancy. *Pediatrics* 29:579-588.

Brazelton, T.B. 1973. *Neonatal behavioral assessment scale. Clinics in developmental medicine* no. 50. Philadelphia: Lippincott.

Brazelton, T.B. 1984. *Neonatal behavioral assessment scale.* 2d ed. Philadelphia: Lippincott.

Brazelton, T.B., Parker, W., Zuckerman, B. 1976. Importance of behavioral assessment in the neonate. *Current Problems in Pediatrics* 2(7):1-82.

Brooks, P.L., & Frost, B.J. 1983. Evaluation of a tactile vocoder for word recognition. *Journal of the Acoustical Society of America* 74:34-39.

Brooks, P.L., Frost, B.J., Mason, J.L., & Gibson, D.M. 1986a. Continuing evaluation of the Queen's University tactile vocoder. I: Identification of open set words. *Journal of Rehabilitation Research and Development* 23:119-128.

Brooks, P.L., Frost, B.J., Mason, J.L., & Gibson, D.M. 1986b. Continuing evaluation of the Queen's University tactile vocoder. II: Identification of open set sentences and tracking narrative. *Journal of Rehabilitation Research and Development* 23:129-138.

Brossard, L.M., & De Carie, T.G. 1968. Comparative reinforcing effect of eight stimulations on the smiling response of infants. *Journal of Child Psychology and Psychiatry* 9:51-59.

Brown, G. Andrews, B., Harris, T., Adler, Z., & Bridge, L. 1986. Social support, self-esteem, and depression. *Psychological Medicine* 16:813-831.

Butcher, E. 1986. The regulation of lymphocyte traffic. *Microbiology and Immunology* 128:85-122.

Casler, L. 1961. Maternal deprivation: A critical review of the literature. *Monographs for Research in Child Development,* 26 no. 2. New York: Child Development Publications.

Chandra, R. 1983. Numerical and functional deficiency in T helper cells in protein energy malnutrition. *Clinical and Experimental Immunology* 51:126-132.

Chisholm, J.S. 1978. Swaddling, cradleboards and development of children. *Early Human Development* 2(3):255-275.

Chu, A., Patterson, J., Goldstein, G., Berger, C., Takezaki, S., & Edelson, R. 1983. Thymopoietin-like substance in human skin. *Journal of Investigative Dermatology* 81:194-197.

Coe, C., Cassayre, P., Levine, S., & Rosenberg, L. 1988. Effects of age, sex, and psychological disturbance on immunoglobulin levels in the squirrel monkey. *Developmental Psychobiology* 21:161-175.

Coe, C., Mendoza, S., Smotherman, W., & Levine, S. 1978. Mother-infant attachment in the squirrel monkey: Adrenal response to separation. *Behavioral Biology* 22:256-263.

Coe, C., Rosenberg, L., Fischer, M., & Levine, S. 1987. Psychological factors capable of preventing the inhibition of antibody responses in separated infant monkeys. *Child Development* 58:1420-1430.

Coe, C., Rosenberg, L., & Levine, S. 1988. Effect of maternal separation on the complement system and antibody responses in infant primates. *International Journal of Neuroscience* 40:289-302.

Cohen, J., & Crnic, L. 1982. Glucocorticoids, stress, and the immune response. In D. Webb (Ed.), *Immunopharmacology and the regulation of leukocyte function.* New York: Marcel Dekker.

Cohen, J., & Crnic, L. 1984. Behavior, stress, and lymphocyte recirculation. In E. Cooper (Ed.), *Stress, aging, and immunity.* New York: Marcel Dekker.

Dallman, M.F., Akana, S., Cascio, C.S., Darlington, D.N., Jacobson, L., & Levin, N. 1987. Regulation of ACTH secretion: Variations on a theme of B. *Recent Progress in Hormone Research* 43:113-173.

Deaux, K. 1985. Sex and gender. *Annual Review of Psychology* 36:49-81.

de Carvalho, M., Klaus, M., & Merkatz, R. 1982. Frequency of breast-feeding and serum bilirubin concentration. *American Journal of Diseases of Children* 136:737-738.

de Carvalho, M., Robertson, S., Friedman, A., & Klaus, M. 1983. Effect of frequent breast-feeding on early milk production and infant weight gain. *Pediatrics* 72:307-311.

deChateau, P. 1976. The influence of early contact on maternal and infant behavior in primiparae. *Birth and Family Journal* 3(4):149-155.

DeKosky, S.T., Scheff, S.W., Cotman, C.W. 1984. Elevated corticosterone levels: A possible cause of reduced axon sprouting in aged animals. *Neuroendocrinology* 38:33-38.

DeLay, T., Kennell, J., & Klaus, M. 1987. Supportive companions of women in labor: A descriptive analysis. Paper presented at the annual meetings of the Society for Research in Child Development, Baltimore.

Donnerer, J., Oka, K., Brossi, A., Rice, K., & Spector, S. 1986. Presence and formation of codeine and morphine in the rat. *Proceedings of the National Academy of Science, U.S.A.* 83:4566-4567.

Dreyfus-Brisac, C. 1970. Ontogenesis of sleep in human prematures after 32 weeks of conceptual age. *Developmental Psychobiology* 3:91-121.

Dreyfus-Brisac, C., & Monod, N. 1975. The electroencephalogram of full-term newborns and premature infants. *Handbook of electroencephalography and clinical neurophysiology* (Vol. 6b). Amsterdam: Elsevier.

Eilers, R.E., Widen, J.E., & Oller, D.K. 1988. Assessment techniques to evaluate tactual aids for hearing-impaired subjects. *Journal of Rehabilitation Research and Development* 25:33-46.

Engelmann, S., & Rosov, R. 1975. Tactual hearing experiment with deaf and hearing subjects. *Exceptional Children* 41:243-253.

Erber, N. 1974. Visual perception of speech by deaf children: Recent developments and continuing needs. *Journal of Speech and Hearing Research* 39:178-185.

Etzel, B., & Gewirtz, J. 1967. Experimental modification of caretaker-maintained high-rate operant crying in a 6- and a 20-week-old infant (*Infans tyrannotearus*): Extinction of crying with reinforcement of eye contact and smiling. *Journal of Experimental Child Psychology* 5:303-317.

Feldman, S., & Conforti, N. 1980. Participation of the dorsal hippocampus in the glucocorticoid negative-feedback effect on adrenocortical activity. *Neuroendocrinology* 30:52-55.

Felten, D., Felten, S., Bellinger, D., Carlson, S., Ackerman, K., Madden, K., Olschowki, J., & Livnat, S. 1987. Noradrenergic sympathetic neural interactions with the immune system: Structure and function. *Immunological Reviews* 100:225-260.

Felten, D., Felten, S., Carlson, S., Olschowki, J., & Livnat, S. 1985. Noradrenergic and peptidergic innervation of lymphoid tissue. *Journal of Immunology* 135:755s-765s.

Field, T., Schanberg, S., Scafidi, F., Bauer, C., Vega-Lahr, N., Garcia, R., Nystrom, J., & Kuhn, C. 1986. Tactile/kinesthetic stimulation effects on preterm neonates. *Pediatrics* 77(5):654-658.

Fischette, C.T., Komisurak, B.R., Ediner, H.M., Feder, H.H., & Siegal, A. 1980. Differential fornix ablations and the circadian rhythmicity of adrenal corticosterone secretion. *Brain Research* 195:373-380.

Fisher, J., Rytting, M., & Heslin, R. 1976. Affective and evaluative effects of an interpersonal touch. *Sociometry* 39:416-421.

Friedman, D., Boverman, H., & Friedman, N. 1966. Effects of kinesthetic stimulation on weight-gain and smiling in premature infants. Paper presented at the meetings of the American Orthopsychiatric Association, San Francisco.

Garbanati, J.A., & Parmelee, A. 1987. State organization in preterm infants: Microanalysis of 24-hour polygraphic recordings. In N. Gunzenhauser (Ed.), *Infant stimulation: For whom, what kind, when, and how much?* Pediatric Round Table: 13. Skillman, N.J.: Johnson & Johnson Baby Products Company.

Gekoski, M., Rovee-Collier, C., & Carulli-Rabinowitz, V. 1983. A longitudinal analysis of inhibition of infant distress: The origins of social expectations? *Infant Behavior and Development* 6:339-351.

Gewirtz, J.L. 1961. A learning analysis of the effects of normal stimulation, privation, and deprivation on the acquisition of social motivation and attachment. In B. Foss (Ed.), *Determinants of infant behaviour.* London: Methuen; New York: Wiley.

Gewirtz, J.L. 1969. Mechanisms of social learning: Some roles of stimulation and behavior in early human development. In D.A. Goslin (Ed.), *Handbook of socialization theory and research.* Chicago: Rand-McNally.

Gewirtz, J.L. 1977. Maternal responding and the conditioning of infant crying: Directions of influence within the attachment-acquisition process. In B.C. Etzel, J.M. LeBlanc, & D.M. Baer (Eds.), *New developments in behavioral research: Theories, methods, and applications*. Hillsdale, N.J.: Erlbaum.

Gewirtz, J.L. In press. Social influence on child and parent behavior via stimulation and operant-learning mechanisms. In M. Lewis & S. Feinman (Eds.), *Social influences on behavior.* New York: Plenum Press.

Gewirtz, J.L., & Boyd, E. 1977. Experiments on mother-infant interaction underlying mutual attachment acquisition: The infant conditions the mother. In T. Alloway, P. Pliner, & L. Krames (Eds.), *Attachment behavior.* New York: Plenum Press.

Gewirtz, J.L., & Pelaez-Nogueras, M. 1987. Social-conditioning theory applied to metaphors like "attachment": The conditioning of infant separation protests by mothers. *Revista Mexicana de Analisis de la Conducta* 13(1 & 2):87-103.

Gewirtz, J.L., & Pelaez-Nogueras, M. 1989. Maternal training of infant protests: Learning to discriminate between departure and separation settings. Paper presented at the biennial meetings of the Society for Research in Child Development, Kansas City, April 27.

Giacoman, S.L. 1971. The effects of hunger and motor restraint on arousal and visual attention in the infant. *Child Development* 42:605-614.

Gibbs, D.M. 1986. Vasopressin and oxytocin: Hypothalamic modulators of the stress response. *Psychoneuroendocrinology* 11:131-140.

Glaser, B., & Strauss, A. 1967. *The discovery of grounded theory.* Chicago: Aldine Press.

Goldman, A.S., & Smith, C.W. 1973. Host resistance factors in human milk. *Journal of Pediatrics* 83:1082-1090.

Goldstein, S., & Field, T. 1985. Affective behavior and weight changes among hospitalized failure-to-thrive infants. *Infant Mental Health Journal* 6:187-194.

Gorski, P., Leonard, C., Sweet, D., Martin, J., Sehring, S., O'Hara, K., High, P., Lang, M., Piecuch, R., & Green, J. 1984. Caring for immature infants: A touchy subject. In C.C. Brown (Ed.), *The many facets of touch,* Pediatric Round Table: 10. Skillman, N.J.: Johnson & Johnson Baby Products Company.

Greenbaum, P., & Rosenfeld, H. 1980. Varieties of touching in greetings: Sequential structure and sex-related differences. *Journal of Nonverbal Behavior* 5:13-25.

Gunnar, M., Gonzalez, C., Goodlin, B., & Levine, S. 1981. Behavioral and pituitary-adrenal responses during a prolonged separation period in infant rhesus macaques. *Psychoneuroendocrinology* 6:65-75.

Gunnar, M., Malone, S., Vance, G., & Fisch, R. 1985. Coping with aversive stimulation in the neonatal period: Quiet sleep and plasma cortisol levels during recovery from circumcision. *Child Development* 56:824-834.

Gyorgy, P. 1967. Human milk and resistance to infection. In *Nutrition and infection*, Ciba Foundation Study Group no. 31. Boston: Little, Brown.

Hall, E. 1966. *The hidden dimension*. New York: Doubleday.

Hasselmayer, E. 1964. The premature neonate's response to handling. *Journal of the American Nursing Association* 11:15-24.

Heidt, P. 1979. *An investigation of the effects of therapeutic touch on anxiety of hospitalized patients*. New York University: Unpublished doctoral dissertation.

Heidt, P. 1981. Effects of therapeutic touch on anxiety level of hospitalized patients. *Nursing Research* 30:32-37.

Heidt, P. 1989. *A qualitative study of nurses' and patients' experiences of therapeutic touch*. Unpublished manuscript.

Henley, N. 1973a. The politics of touch. In P. Brown (Ed.), *Radical psychology*. New York: Harper & Row.

Henley, N. 1973b. Status and sex: Some touching observations. *Bulletin of the Psychonomic Society* 2:91-93.

Henley, N. 1977. *Body politics: Power, sex and nonverbal communication.* Englewood Cliffs, N.J.: Prentice-Hall.

Hennessy, M., Kaplan, J., Mendoza, S., Lowe, E., & Levine, S. 1979. Separation distress and attachment in surrogate-reared squirrel monkeys. *Physiology and Behavior* 23:1017-1023.

Heslin, R. 1976. *Attraction in the dyad.* Unpublished manuscript, Purdue University.

Heslin, R., & Boss, D. 1980. Nonverbal intimacy in airport arrival and departure. *Personality and Social Psychology Bulletin* 6:248-252.

Hess, J.L., Denenberg, V.H., Zarrow, M.X., & Pfeifer, W.D. 1969. Modification of the corticosterone response curve as a function of handling in infancy. *Physiology and Behavior* 4:109-112.

Hoffman, L. 1972. Early childhood experiences and women's achievement motives. *Journal of Social Issues* 28:157-176.

Hopkins, B. 1976. Culturally determined patterns of handling the human infant. *Journal of Human Movement Studies* 2:1.

Hunziker, U., & Barr, R. 1986. Increased carrying reduces infant crying: A randomized controlled trial. *Pediatrics* 77:641-648.

Irwin, J., & Livnat, S. 1987. Behavioral influences on the immune system: Stress and conditioning. *Progress in Neuropsychopharmacology and Biological Psychiatry* 11:137-143.

Issa, A., Rowe, W., Gauthier, S., & Meaney, M.J. Hypothalamic-pituitary-adrenal function in cognitively impaired and unimpaired aged rats. Manuscript submitted for publication.

Jansch, E. 1980. *The self-organizing universe: Scientific and human implications of the emerging paradigm of evolution.* Oxford: Pergamon Press.

Jay, S. 1982. *The effects of gentle human touch on mechanically ventilated very short gestation infants.* University of Pittsburgh: Unpublished doctoral dissertation.

Jelliffe, D.B., & Jelliffe, E.F.P. 1971. The uniqueness of human milk. *American Journal of Clinical Nutrition* 24:968-969.

Johnson, J., Leventhal, H., & Dabbs, J., Jr. 1971. Contribution of emotional and instrumental processes in adaptation to surgery. *Journal of Personality and Social Psychology* 20:55-64.

Jones, M.T., Gillham, B., Greenstein, B.D., Beckford, U., & Holmes, M.C. 1982. Feedback actions of adrenal steroid hormones. In D. Ganten & D. Pfaff (Eds.), *Current topics in neuroendocrinology,* vol. 2. New York: Springer.

Jourard, S. 1966. An exploratory study of body accessibility. *British Journal of Social and Clinical Psychology* 5:221-231.

Jourard, S., & Rubin, J. 1968. Self-disclosure and touching: A study of two modes of interpersonal encounter and their interrelation. *Journal of Humanistic Psychology* 8:39-48.

Kaitz, M., Eidelman, A., Lapidot, P., Bonner, R., Segal, D. 1989. Postpartum women can recognize their infants by touch. *Pediatric Research* 25:14A.

Kakar, S. 1978. *The inner world*. New York: Oxford University Press.

Kakar, S. 1979. *Indian childhood: Cultural ideals and social reality*. London: Oxford University Press.

Kattwinkle, J., Nearman, H., Fanaroff, A., Katona, P., & Klaus, M. 1975. Apnea of prematurity: Comparative therapeutic effects of cutaneous stimulation and nasal continuous positive airway pressure. *Journal of Pediatrics* 86(4):588-592.

Kaufman, I., & Rosenblum, L. 1969. Effects of separation from mother on the emotional behavior of infant monkeys. *Annals of the New York Academy of Science* 159:681-695.

Keller, E., & Bzdek, V. 1986. Effects of therapeutic touch on tension headache pain. *Nursing Research* 35:101-104.

Keller-Wood, M., & Dallman, M.F. 1984. Corticosteroid inhibition of ACTH secretion. *Endocrine Reviews* 5:1-24.

Kennell, J., Klaus, M., McGrath, S., Robertson, S., & Hinkley, C. 1988. Medical interventions: The effect of social support during labor. *Pediatric Research* 61:211A.

Kirman, J. 1973. Tactile communication of speech: A review and an analysis. *Psychological Bulletin* 80:54-74.

Klaus, M., Jerauld, R., Kreger, N., McAlpine, W., Steffa, M., & Kennell, J. 1972. Maternal attachment: Importance of the first post-partum days. *New England Journal of Medicine* 286:460-463.

Klaus, M., & Kennell, J. 1982. *Parent-infant bonding* (2d ed.). St. Louis: Mosby.

Klaus, M., Kennell, J., Plumb, B., & Zuehlke, S. 1970. Human maternal behavior at the first contact with her young. *Pediatrics* 46:187-192.

Klaus, M., Kennell, J., Robertson, S., & Sosa, R. 1986. Effects of social support during parturition on maternal and infant morbidity. *British Medical Journal* 293:585-587.

Kleinke, C. 1977. Compliance to requests made by gazing and touching experimenters in field settings. *Journal of Experimental Social Psychology* 13:218-223.

Konner, M. 1976. Maternal care, infant behavior and development among the !Kung. In R. Lee & I. DeVore (Eds.), *Kalahari hunter-gatherers: Studies of the !Kung San and their neighbors*. Cambridge: Harvard University Press.

Konner, M. 1981. Evolution of human behavior development. In R.L. Munroe, R.H. Munroe, & B. Whiting (Eds.), *Handbook of cross-cultural human development.* New York: Garland.

Korner, A.F., & Thoman, E.B. 1972. The relative efficacy of contact and vestibular-proprioceptive stimulation in soothing neonates. *Child Development* 43:443-453.

Kramer, M., Chamorro, I., Green, D., & Knudtson, F. 1975. Extra tactile stimulation of the premature infant. *Nursing Research* 24:324-334.

Krauss, K. 1987. The effects of deep pressure touch in anxiety. *American Journal of Occupational Therapy* 41:366-373.

Krieger, D. 1974. Healing by the laying-on of hands as a facilitator of bioenergetic change: The response of in-vivo human hemoglobin. *Psychoenergetics* 1:121-129.

Krieger, D. 1979. *Therapeutic touch: How to use your hands to help and heal.* Englewood Cliffs, N.J.: Prentice-Hall.

Krozowski, Z.S., & Funder, J.W. 1983. Renal mineralocorticoid receptors and hippocampal corticosterone binding species have intrinsic steroid specificity. *Proceedings of the National Academy of Science, U.S.A.* 80:6056-6060.

Lagercrantz, H., & Slotkin, T. 1986. The "stress" of being born. *Scientific American* 254:100-107.

Lamb, M., & Malkin, C. 1986. The development of social expectations in distress-relief sequences: A longitudinal study. *International Journal of Behavior and Development* 9:235-249.

Landers, C. 1983. Biological, social, and cultural determinants of infant behavior in a South Indian fishing village. Harvard University Graduate School of Education: unpublished doctoral dissertation.

Landfield, P., Baskin, R.K., & Pitler, T.A. 1981. Brain-aging correlates: Retardation by hormonal-pharmacological treatments. *Science* 214:581-583.

Landfield, P., Waymire, J., & Lynch, G. 1978. Hippocampal aging and adrenocorticoids: A quantitative correlation. *Science* 202:1098:1101.

Laudenslager, M. 1988. The psychobiology of loss: Lessons from humans and nonhuman primates. *Journal of Sociological Issues* 44:19-36.

Laudenslager, M., Capitanio, J., & Reite, M. 1985. Some possible consequences of early separation experiences on subsequent immune function. *American Journal of Psychiatry* 142:862-864.

Laudenslager, M., Reite, M., & Harbeck, R. 1982. Suppressed immune response in infant monkeys associated with maternal separation. *Behavioral and Neural Biology* 36:40-48.

Laudenslager, M., Reite, M., & Held, P. 1986. Early mother-infant separation experiences impair the primary but not the secondary antibody response to a novel antigen in young pigtail monkeys. *Psychosomatic Medicine* 48:304.

Leboyer, F. 1976. *Loving hands.* New York: Knopf.

Lester, B.M., Als, H., & Brazelton, T.B. 1982. Regional obstetric anesthesia and newborn behavior: A reanalysis toward synergistic effects. *Child Development* 53:687-692.

Lester, B. M., & Brazelton, T.B. 1982. Cross-cultural assessment of neonatal behavior. In D.A. Wagner & H.W. Stevenson (Eds.), *Cultural perspectives on child development.* San Francisco: W.H. Freeman.

LeVine, R.A. 1977. Child rearing as cultural adaptation. In H. Leiderman, S. Tulkin, & A. Rosenfeld (Eds.), *Culture and infancy.* New York: Academic Press.

Levine, S. 1957. Infantile experience and resistance to physiological stress. *Science* 126:405-406.

Levine, S. 1962. Plasma-free corticosteroid response to electric shock in rats stimulated in infancy. *Science* 135:795-796.

Lewin, M., & Goldberg, S. 1969. Perceptual-cognitive development in infancy: A generalized expectancy model as a function of the mother-infant relationship. *Merrill-Palmer Quarterly* 15:81.

Lionberger, H. 1985. *An interpretive study of nurses' practice of therapeutic touch.* University of California, San Francisco: Unpublished doctoral dissertation.

Lipton, E.L., Steinschneider, A., & Richmond, J.B. 1965. Swaddling, a child care practice: Historical, cultural, and experimental observations. *Pediatrics* (Suppl.) 35:521.

Livnat, S., Felten, S., Carlson, S., Bellinger, D., & Felten, D. 1985. Involvement of peripheral and central catecholamine systems in neural-immune interactions. *Journal of Neuroimmunology* 10:5-30.

Long, J., Philip, A., & Lucey, J. 1980. Excessive handling as a cause of hypoxemia. *Pediatrics* 65:203-206.

Lowrey, G.H. 1973. *Growth and development of children*. Chicago: Yearbook Medical Publishers.

Lozoff, B. 1983. Birth and "bonding" in non-industrial societies. *Developmental Medicine and Child Neurology* 25:595-600.

Lozoff, B., & Brittenham, G. 1979. Infant care: Cache or carry. *Journal of Pediatrics* 95:475-483.

Lozoff, B., Brittenham, G., Trause, M., Kennell, J., & Klaus, M. 1977. The mother-newborn relationship: Limits of adaptability. *Journal of Pediatrics* 91:1-12.

Lynch, M.P., Eilers, R.E., Oller, D.K., & LaVoie, L. 1988. Speech perception by congenitally deaf subjects using an electrocutaneous vocoder. *Journal of Rehabilitation Research and Development* 25(3):41-50.

Lynch, M.P., Eilers, R.E., Oller, D.K., Urbano, R.C., & Pero, P.J. 1989. Multisensory narrative tracking by a profoundly deaf subject using an electrocutaneous vocoder and a vibrotactile aid. *Journal of Speech and Hearing Research* 32:331-338.

Maccoby, E. (Ed.). 1966. *The development of sex differences*. Stanford, Calif.: Stanford University Press.

Maier, S., & Laudenslager, M. 1988. Commentary: Inescapable shock, shock controllability and mitogen stimulated lymphocyte proliferation. *Brain, Behavior, and Immunity* 2:87-91.

Major, B., & Heslin, R. 1982. Perceptions of cross-sex and same-sex nonreciprocal touch: It is better to give than to receive. *Journal of Nonverbal Behavior* 6:148-162.

Martin, B. 1961. The assessment of anxiety by physiological and behavioral measures. *Psychological Bulletin* 58:234-255.

Mata, L.J. 1978. *The children of Santa Maria Cauque: A prospective field study of health and growth*. Cambridge: MIT Press.

Mata, L.J., & Wyatt, R.G. 1971. The uniqueness of human milk. *American Journal of Clinical Nutrition* 24:976-986.

McClure, V.S. 1989. *Infant massage: A handbook for loving parents* (rev. ed.). New York: Bantam Books.

McEwen, B.S., DeKloet, E.R., & Rostene, W.H. 1986. Adrenal steroid receptors and actions in the nervous system. *Physiology Reviews* 66:1121-1150.

McGrady, A., Younker, R., Tan, S., Fine, T., & Woerner, M. 1981. The effect of biofeedback assisted relaxation training. *Biofeedback and Self Regulation* 6:343-353.

McLean, P., & Hakistian, R. 1979. Clinical depression: Comparative efficacy of outpatient treatments. *Journal of Consulting and Clinical Psychology* 47:818-836.

McNair, D., Lorr, M., & Droppleman, L. 1971. *Profile of mood states manual.* San Diego: Educational and Industrial Testing Services.

Meaney, M.J., & Aitken, D.H. 1985. The effects of early postnatal handling on the development of hippocampal glucocorticoid receptors: Temporal parameters. *Developmental Brain Research* 22:301-304.

Meaney, M.J., Aitken, D.H., Bhatnagar, S., & Sapolsky, R.M. In press. Environmental regulation of the adrenocortical stress response in female rats: Implications for individual differences in aging. *Neurobiology of Aging.*

Meaney, M.J., Aitken, D.H., Bhatnagar, S., Van Berkel, C., & Sapolsky, R.M. 1988. Postnatal handling attenuates neuroendocrine, anatomical, and cognitive impairments related to the aged hippocampus. *Science* 238:766-768.

Meaney, M.J., Aitken, D.H., Bodnoff, S.R., Iny, L.J., & Sapolsky, R.M. 1985. The effects of postnatal handling on the development of the glucocorticoid receptor systems and stress recovery in the rat. *Progress in Neuropsychopharmacology and Biological Psychiatry* 7:731-734.

Meaney, M.J., Aitken, D.H., Bodnoff, S.R., Iny, L.J., Tatarewicz, J.E., & Sapolsky, R.M. 1985. Early, postnatal handling alters glucocorticoid receptor concentrations in selected brain regions. *Behavioral Neuroscience* 99:760-765.

Meaney, M.J., Aitken, D.H., & Sapolsky, R.M. 1987. Thyroid hormones influence the development of hippocampal glucocorticoid receptors in the rat: A mechanism for the effects of postnatal handling on the development of the adrenocortical stress response. *Neuroendocrinology* 45:278-283.

Meaney, M.J., Aitken, D.H., Sharma, S., & Viau, V. In press. Basal ACTH, corticosterone, and corticosterone-binding globulin levels over the diurnal cycle, and hippocampal type I and type II corticosteroid receptors in young and old, handled and nonhandled rats. *Neuroendocrinology.*

Meaney, M.J., Aitken, D.H., Sharma, S., Viau, V., & Sarrieau, A. 1989. Postnatal handling increases hippocampal type II, glucocorticoid receptors and enhances adrenocortical negative-feedback efficacy in the rat. *Neuroendocrinology* 50:597-604.

Meaney, M.J., Viau, V., Bhatnagar, S., & Aitken, D.H. 1988. Occupancy and translocation of hippocampal glucocorticoid receptors during and following stress. *Brain Research* 445:198-203.

Meehan, T. 1985. *The effect of therapeutic touch on the experience of acute pain in postoperative patients.* New York University: Unpublished doctoral dissertation.

Mendoza, S., Smotherman, W., Miner, M., Kaplan, J., & Levine, S. 1978. Pituitary-adrenal response to separation in mother and infant squirrel monkeys. *Developmental Psychobiology* 11:169-175.

Mitchell, J.B., Iny, L.J., & Meaney, M.J. In press. The role of serotonin in the developmental and environmental regulation of hippocampal type II corticosteroid receptors. *Developmental Brain Research.*

Mitchell, J.B., Rowe, W., Boksa, P., & Meaney, M.J. In press. Serotonin regulates type II corticosteroid receptor binding in hippocampal cell cultures. *Journal of Neuroscience.*

Mittelman, G., & Valenstein, E. 1984. Ingestive behavior evoked by hypothalamic stimulation and schedule-induced polydipsia are related. *Science* 224:415-417.

Moldofsky, H., Lue, F., Eisen, J., Keystone, E., & Gorczynski, R. 1986. The relationship of interleukin-1 and immune functions to sleep in humans. *Psychosomatic Medicine* 48:309-318.

Morris, R.G.M., Garrard, P., Rawlins, J.N.P., O'Keefe, J. 1982. Place navigation impairment in rats with hippocampal lesions. *Nature* 297:681-683.

Munck, A., Guyre, P.M., & Holbrook, N.J. 1984. Physiological functions of glucocorticoids in stress and their relations to pharmacological actions. *Endocrine Reviews* 5:25-44.

Murray, A. 1979. Infant crying as an elicitor of parental behavior: An examination of two models. *Psychological Bulletin* 86:191-215.

Musaph, H. 1978. The skin as an organ of communication. *Hexagon* 1:8-13.

Nagashima, L., Bertsch, T., Dykeman, S., McGrath, S., DeLay, T., & Kennell, J. 1987. Fathers during labor: Do we expect too much? *Pediatric Research* 21:62.

Newman, L. 1982. The special care nursery: An anthropological study. In M.H. Klaus & M.O. Robertson (Eds.), *Birth, interaction and attachment,* Pediatric Round Table: 6. Skillman, N.J.: Johnson & Johnson Baby Products Company.

New York State Department of Education. 1988. *Bonding and relaxation techniques.* Title VI-C, Grant #101115-3H-88. Albany: New York State Department of Education.

Nguyen, T., Heslin, R., & Nguyen, M. 1975. The meaning of touch: Sex differences. *Journal of Communication* 25:92-103.

Nijhuis, J., Prechtl, H., Martin, C., & Bots, R. 1982. Are there behavioural states in the human fetus? *Early Human Development* 6:177-195.

Older, J. 1982. *Touching is healing.* New York: Stein and Day.

Older, J. 1984. Teaching touch at medical school. *Journal of the American Medical Association* 252:931-933.

Oller, D.K. 1986. Metaphonology and infant vocalizations. In B. Lindblom & R. Zetterstrom (Eds.), *Precursors of early speech.* New York: Stockton Press.

Oller, D.K., & Eilers, R.E. 1988. Tactual artificial hearing for the deaf. In F. Bess (Ed.), *Hearing impairment in children.* Parkton, Md.: York Press.

Orne, M. 1962. On the social psychology of the psychological experiment: With particular reference to demand characteristics and their implications. *American Psychologist* 17:776-783.

Ozdamar, O., Oller, D.K., Miskiel, E., & Eilers, R.E. 1988. Computer system for quantitative evaluation of an electrotactile vocoder for artificial hearing. *Computers and Biomedical Research* 21:85-100.

Parkes, B. 1985. *Therapeutic touch as an intervention to reduce anxiety in elderly hospitalized patients.* University of Texas, Austin: Unpublished doctoral dissertation.

Patterson, M. 1976. An arousal model of interpersonal intimacy. *Psychological Review* 83:235-245.

Pickett, J.M., & Pickett, B.H. 1963. Communication of speech sounds by a tactual vocoder. *Journal of Speech and Hearing Research* 5:207-222.

Platania, A., Field, T., Blank, J., & Seligman, F. 1989. Relaxation therapy reduces anxiety in child/adolescent psychiatry patients. Manuscript submitted for publication.

Plooij, F. 1984. *The behavioral development of free-living chimpanzee babies and infants.* Norwood, N.J.: Ablex.

Plotsky, P.M., Otto, S., & Sapolsky, R.M. 1986. Inhibition of immunoreactive corticotropin-releasing factor into the hypophysial-portal circulation by delayed glucocorticoid feedback. *Endocrinology* 119:1126-1130.

Plotsky, P.M., & Vale, W.W. 1984. Hemorrhage-induced secretion of corticotropin-releasing factor-like immunoreactivity into the rat hypophysial-portal circulation and its inhibition by glucocorticoids. *Endocrinology* 114:164-169.

Powell, G., Brasel, J., & Blizzard, R. 1967. Emotional deprivation and growth retardation simulating idiopathic hypopituitarism: Clinical evaluation of the syndrome. *New England Journal of Medicine* 276:1271-1278.

Powell, G., Brasel, J., Raiti, S., & Blizzard, R. 1967. Emotional deprivation and growth retardation simulating idiopathic hypopituitarism. II. Endocrinologic evaluation of the syndrome. *New England Journal of Medicine* 276:1279-1283.

Prechtl, H.F., & Beintema, D. 1964. *The neurological examination of the full-term newborn infant.* London: Heinemann.

Quinn, J. 1984. Therapeutic touch as energy exchange: Testing the theory. *Advances in Nursing Science* 6:42-49.

Rausch, P. 1981a. Effects of tactile and kinesthetic stimulation on premature infants. *Journal of Obstetric, Gynecologic, and Neonatal Nursing* 10:34-37.

Rausch, P. 1981b. Neurophysiological development in premature infants following stimulation. *Developmental Psychology* 13:69-76.

Reite, M. 1984. Touch, attachment, and health — Is there a relationship? In C.C. Brown (Ed.), *The many facets of touch.* Pediatric Round Table: 10. Skillman, N.J.: Johnson & Johnson Baby Products Company.

Reite, M. 1985. Implantable biotelemetry and social separation in monkeys. In G. Moberg (Ed.), *Animal stress.* Bethesda, Md.: American Physiological Society.

Reite, M., & Capitanio, J. 1985. On the nature of social separation and social attachment. In M. Reite & T. Field (Eds.), *The psychobiology of attachment and separation.* Orlando, Fla.: Academic Press.

Reite, M., Harbeck, R., & Hoffman, S. 1981. Altered cellular immune response following maternal separation. *Life Sciences* 28:1133-1136.

Reite, M., Kaemingk, K., & Boccia, M. 1989. Maternal separation in bonnet monkey infants: Altered attachment and social support. *Child Development* 60:473-480.

Reite, M., Laudenslager, M., Jones, J., Crnic, L., & Kaemingk, K. 1987. Interferon decreases REM latency. *Biological Psychiatry* 22:104-107.

Reite, M., Seiler, C., Crowley, T., Hydinger-MacDonald, M., & Short, R. 1982. Circadian rhythm changes following maternal separation in monkeys. *Chronobiologia* 9:1-11.

Reite, M., Seiler, C., & Short, R. 1978. Loss of your mother is more than loss of a mother. *American Journal of Psychiatry* 135:370-371.

Reite, M., & Short, R. 1978. Nocturnal sleep in separated monkey infants. *Archives of General Psychiatry* 35:1247-1253.

Reite, M., Short, R., Kaufman, I.C., Stynes, A.J., & Pauley, J.D. 1978. Heart rate and body temperature in separated monkey infants. *Biological Psychiatry* 13:91-105.

Reite, M., Short, R., Seiler, C., & Pauley, J. 1981. Attachment, loss and depression. *Journal of Child Psychology and Psychiatry* 22:141-169.

Reul, J.M., & DeKloet, E.R. 1985. Two receptor systems for corticosterone in rat brain: Microdistribution and differential occupation. *Endocrinology* 117:2505-2511.

Reul, J.M., Tonnaer, J., & DeKloet, E.R. 1988. Neurotrophic ACTH analogue promotes plasticity of type I corticosteroid receptors in brain of senescent male rats. *Neurobiology of Aging* 9:253-257.

Reul, J.M., van den Bosch, F.R., & DeKloet, E.R. 1987. Differential response of type I and type II corticosteroid receptors to changes in plasma steroid levels and circadian rhythmicity. *Neuroendocrinology* 45:407-412.

Reynolds, W., & Coats, K. 1986. A comparison of cognitive-behavioral therapy and relaxation training for treatment of depression in adolescents. *Journal of Consulting and Clinical Psychology* 54:653-660.

Rheingold, H., Gewirtz, J., & Ross, H. 1959. Social conditioning of vocalizations in the infant. *Journal of Comparative and Physiological Psychology* 52:68-73.

Rice, R. 1979. The effects of the Rice sensorimotor stimulation treatment on the development of high risk infants. *Birth Defects Original Article Series* 15:7-26. New York: Alan R. Liss.

Richter, N. 1984. The efficacy of relaxation therapy with children. *Journal of Abnormal Child Psychology* 12:319-344.

Ritger, H., Veldhuis, H.D., & DeKloet, E.R. 1984. Spatial orientation and hippocampal corticosterone receptor systems of old rats: Effects of ACTH4-9 analogue ORG2766. *Brain Research* 309:393-399.

Rivier, C., Brownstein, M., Spiess, J., Rivier, J., & Vale, W. 1982. In vivo corticotropin-releasing factor-induced secretion of adrenocorticotropin, beta-endorphin, and corticosterone. *Endocrinology* 110:272-278.

Rivier, C., & Plotsky, P.M. 1986. Mediation by corticotropin-releasing factor of adenohypophysial hormone secretion. *Annals of the Review of Physiology* 48:475-489.

Rivier, C., & Vale, W.W. 1983. Effects of angiotensin II on ACTH release in vivo: Role of corticotropin-releasing factor (CRF). *Regulatory Peptides* 7:253-258.

Roger, L., Schanberg, S., & Fellows, R. 1974. Growth and lactogenic hormone stimulation of ornithine decarboxylase in neonatal rat brain. *Endocrinology* 95:904-911.

Rogers, M. 1970. *An introduction to the theoretical basis of nursing.* Philadelphia: F.A. Davis.

Rosenblum, L., & Kaufman, I. 1967. Laboratory observations of early mother-infant relations in pigtail and bonnet monkeys. In S. Altman (Ed.), *Social communication among primates.* Chicago: University of Chicago Press.

Rubenfeld, M., Silverstone, A., Knowles, D., Halper, J., DeSostos, A., Fenoglio, C., & Edelson, R. 1981. Induction of lymphocyte differentiation by epidermal cell cultures. *Journal of Investigative Dermatology* 77:221-224.

Sameroff, A. 1975. Early influences on development: Fact or fancy? *Merrill-Palmer Quarterly* 21:267.

Sapolsky, R.M., Krey, L.C., & McEwen, B.S. 1983a. Corticosterone receptors decline in a site-specific manner in the aged rat. *Brain Research* 289:235-240.

Sapolsky, R.M., Krey, L.C., & McEwen, B.S. 1983b. The adrenocortical response in the aged rat: Impairment of recovery from stress. *Journal of Experimental Gerontology* 18:55-63.

Sapolsky, R.M., Krey, L.C., & McEwen, B.S. 1984. Glucocorticoid-sensitive hippocampal neurons are involved in terminating the adrenocortical stress response. *Proceedings of the National Academy of Science* 81:6174-6177.

Sapolsky, R.M., Krey, L.C., & McEwen, B.S. 1985. Prolonged glucocorticoid exposure reduced hippocampal neuron number: Implications for aging. *Journal of Neuroscience* 5:1221-1226.

Sapolsky, R.M., Krey, L.C., & McEwen, B.S. 1986. The neuroendocrinology of stress and aging: The glucocorticoid cascade hypothesis. *Endocrine Reviews* 7:284-301.

Sarrieau, A., Dussaillant, M., Sapolsky, R.M., Aitken, D.H., Olivier, O., Lal, S., Rostene, W.H., Quirion, R., & Meaney, M.J. 1988. Glucocorticoid binding sites in human temporal cortex. *Brain Research* 442:150-154.

Sarrieau, A., Sharma, S., & Meaney, M.J. 1988. Postnatal development and environmental regulation of hippocampal glucocorticoid and mineralocorticoid receptors in the rat. *Developmental Brain Research* 43:158-162.

Sauder, D. 1983. Immunology of the epidermis: Changing perspectives (editorial). *Journal of Investigative Dermatology* 81:185-186.

Scafidi, F., Field, T., Schanberg, S., Bauer, C., Tucci, K., Roberts, J., Morrow, C., & Kuhn, C. M. In press. Massage stimulates growth in preterm infants: A replication. *Infant Behavior and Development*.

Scafidi, F., Field, T., Schanberg, S., Bauer, C., Vega-Lahr, N., Garcia, R., Poirier, J., Nystrom, G., & Kuhn, C. 1986. Effects of tactile/kinesthetic stimulation on the clinical course and sleep/wake behavior of preterm neonates. *Infant Behavior and Development* 9:91-105.

Scarr-Salapatek, S., & Williams, M. 1973. The effects of early stimulation on low birthweight infants. *Child Development* 44:94-101.

Schanberg, S., & Field, T. 1987. Sensory deprivation stress and supplemental stimulation in the rat pup and preterm human neonate. *Child Development* 58:1431-1447.

Schanberg, S., & Field, T. 1988. Maternal deprivation and supplemental stimulation. In T. Field, P. McCabe, & N. Schneiderman (Eds.), *Stress and coping across development*. Hillsdale, N.J.: Erlbaum.

Schmitt, B. 1985. Colic: Excessive crying in newborns. *Clinics in Perinatology* 12:441-451.

Schneider, V. 1988. *Infant massage instructor's manual.* Portland, Oreg.: International Association of Infant Massage Instructors.

Scott, S., Cole, T., Lucas, P., & Richards, M. 1983. Weight gain and movement patterns of very low birthweight babies nursed on lambswool. *Lancet* 2:1014-1016.

Selye, H. 1950. *The physiology and pathology of exposure to stress.* Montreal: Acta.

Sigman, M., & Parmelee, A. 1989, January. Longitudinal predictors of cognitive development. Paper presented at the meetings of the American Association for the Advancement of Science, San Francisco.

Smith, D., Willis, F., & Gier, J. 1980. Success and interpersonal touch in a competitive setting. *Journal of Nonverbal Behavior* 5:26-34.

Smith, E., & Blalock, J. 1988. A molecular basis for interactions between the immune and neuroendocrine systems. *International Journal of Neuroscience* 38:455-464.

Smotherman, W., Hunt, L., McGinnis, L., & Levine, S. 1979. Mother-infant separation in group-living rhesus macaques: A hormonal analysis. *Developmental Psychobiology* 12:211-217.

Solkoff, N., & Matuszak, D. 1975. Tactile stimulation and behavioral development among low-birthweight infants. *Child Psychiatry and Human Development* 6:33-37.

Solkoff, N., Yaffe, S., Weintraub, D., & Blase, B. 1969. Effects of handling on the subsequent development of premature infants. *Developmental Psychology* 1:756-768.

Solomon, G., Levine, E., & Kraft, J. 1968. Early experience and immunity. *Nature* 220:821-822.

Sosa, R., Kennell, J., Klaus, M., Robertson, S., & Urrutia, J. 1980. The effect of a supportive companion on perinatal problems, length of labor, and mother-infant interaction. *New England Journal of Medicine* 303:597-600.

Sparks, D.W., Kuhl, P.K., Edmonds, A.E., & Gray, G.P. 1978. Investigating the MESA (Multipoint Electrotactile Speech Aid): The transmission of segmental features of speech. *Journal of the Acoustical Society of America* 63:246-257.

Spielberger, C., Gorsuch, R., & Lushene, R. 1970. *Manual for the state-trait anxiety inventory.* Palo Alto, Calif.: Consulting Psychologists Press.

Stein, A., & Bailey, M. 1973. The socialization of achievement orientation in females. *Psychological Bulletin* 80:345-366.

Stier, D.S., & Hall, J.A. 1984. Gender differences in touch: An empirical and theoretical review. *Journal of Personality and Social Psychology* 47:440-459.

Stohiar, O.A., Pelley, R.P., Kaniecki-Green, E., Klaus, M.H., & Carpenter, C.C. 1976. Secretory IgA against enterotoxins in breast milk. *Lancet* 1:1258-1261.

Streilein, J. 1983. Lymphocyte traffic, T-cell malignancies and the skin. *Journal of Investigative Dermatology* 71:167-171.

Sullivan, R.M., Wilson, D.A., & Leon, M. 1988. Changes in rat pups' body temperature associated with tactile stimuli. *Developmental Psychobiology* 21:225-236.

Super, C.M. 1981a. Behavioral development in infancy. In R.H. Munroe, R.L. Munroe, & B.B. Whiting (Eds.), *Handbook of cross-cultural human development.* New York: Garland Press.

Super, C.M. 1981b. Cross-cultural research in infancy. In H.C. Triandis & A. Heron (Eds.), *Handbook of cross-cultural psychology: Developmental psychology* (Vol. 4). Boston: Allyn and Bacon.

Tang, G., & Philips, R. 1978. Some age-related changes in pituitary-adrenal function in the male laboratory rat. *Gerontology* 33:377.

Thoman, E. 1975a. Early development of sleeping behaviors in infants. In N. Ellis (Ed.), *Aberrant development in infancy: Human and animal studies.* New York: Wiley.

Thoman, E. 1975b. How a rejecting baby affects mother-infant synchrony. In *Parent-infant interaction,* Ciba Foundation Symposium 33. Amsterdam: Elsevier.

Thomas, L. 1983. *The youngest science: Notes of a medicine watcher.* New York: Viking Press.

Tronick, E.Z. 1987. Prologue to N. Gunzenhauser (Ed.), *Infant stimulation: For whom, what kind, when, and how much?* Pediatric Round Table: 13. Skillman, N.J.: Johnson & Johnson Baby Products Company.

Tronick, E.Z., Morelli, G.A., & Winn, S. 1987. Multiple caretaking of Efe (pygmy) infants. *American Anthropologist* 89:96-106.

Uvnäs-Moberg, K., Widström, A., Marchini, G., & Windberg, J. 1987. Release of GI hormones in mother and infant by sensory stimulation. *Acta Paediatrica Scandinavica* 76:851-860.

Van Loon, G.R., & De Souza, E.B. 1987. Regulation of stress-induced secretion of POMC-derived peptides. *Annals of the New York Academy of Science* 512:300-307.

Walker, D. 1971. Openness to touching: A study of strangers in nonverbal interaction. *Dissertation Abstracts International* 32:574 (University Microfilms no. 71-18, 454).

Weisenberger, J.M. 1988. Effects of number of channels on speech perception with tactile aids. *Journal of the Acoustical Society of America* 84(Suppl. 1):S46.

Weisenberger, J.M., Broadstone, S.M., & Saunders, F.A. 1989. Evaluation of two multichannel tactile aids for the hearing impaired. *Journal of the Acoustical Society of America* 86:1764-1775.

Weisenberger, J.M., & Miller, J.D. 1987. The role of tactile aids in providing information about acoustic stimuli. *Journal of the Acoustical Society of America* 82:906-916.

Wessel, M., Cobb, J., Jackson, E., Harris, G., & Detwiler, A. 1954. Paroxysmal fussing in infancy, sometimes called "colic." *Pediatrics* 14:421-434.

White, J., & Labarba, R. 1976. The effects of tactile and kinesthetic stimulation on neonatal development in the premature infant. *Developmental Psychobiology* 6:569-577.

Willis, F., & Hofmann, G. 1975. Development of tactile patterns in relationship to age, sex, and race. *Developmental Psychology* 11:866.

Willis, F., & Reeves, D. 1976. Touch interactions in junior high school students in relation to sex and race. *Developmental Psychology* 12:91-92.

Willis, F., Reeves, D., & Buchanan, D. 1976. Interpersonal touch in high school relative to sex and race. *Perceptual and Motor Skills* 43:843-847.

Yarrow, L., Rubenstein, J., & Pedersen, F. 1975. *Infant and environment: Early cognitive and motivational development.* New York: Wiley.

Young, V., & Torun, B. 1981. Physical activity: Impact on protein and amino acid metabolism and implications for nutritional requirements. In *Nutrition in health and disease and international development.* Symposia from the XII International Congress of Nutrition. New York: Alan R. Liss.

Zarrow, M.X., Campbel, P.S., & Denenberg, V.H. 1972. Handling in infancy: Increased levels of the hypothalamic corticotropin releasing factor (CRF) following exposure to a novel situation. *Proceedings of the Society of Experimental Biology and Medicine* 356:141-143.